To

_____

From

_____

Date

_____

FAMILY
CHRISTIAN
PRESS

ABOVE ALL ELSE
Directions for life

MEN

Above all else, guard your heart, for it affects everything you do.
Proverbs 4:23-27 NLT

Scripture quotations are taken from:

The Holy Bible, King James Version

The Holy Bible, New International Version (NIV) Copyright © 1973, 1978, 1984, by International Bible Society. Used by permission of Zondervan Publishing House. All rights reserved.

The New American Standard Bible®, (NASB) Copyright © 1960, 1962, 1963, 1968, 1971, 1972, 1973, 1975, 1977, 1995 by The Lockman Foundation. Used by permission.

The Holy Bible, New King James Version (NKJV) Copyright © 1982 by Thomas Nelson, Inc. Used by permission.

The Holy Bible, New Living Translation, (NLT) Copyright © 1996. Used by permission of Tyndale House Publishers, Inc., Wheaton, Illinois 60189. All rights reserved.

New Century Version®. (NCV) Copyright © 1987, 1988, 1991 by Word Publishing, a division of Thomas Nelson, Inc. All rights reserved. Used by permission.

The Holy Bible: Revised Standard Version (RSV). Copyright 1946, 1952, 1959, 1973 by the Division of Christian Education of the National Council of the Churches of Christ in the United States of America. All rights reserved. Used by permission.

The Holy Bible, The Living Bible (TLB), Copyright © 1971 owned by assignment by Illinois Regional Bank N.A. (as trustee). Used by permission of Tyndale House Publishers, Inc., Wheaton, Illinois 60189. All rights reserved.

The Message (MSG) This edition issued by contractual arrangement with NavPress, a division of The Navigators, U.S.A. Originally published by NavPress in English as THE MESSAGE: The Bible in Contemporary Language copyright 2002-2003 by Eugene Peterson. All rights reserved.

The Holman Christian Standard Bible™ (HOLMAN CSB) Copyright © 1999, 2000, 2001 by Holman Bible Publishers. Used by permission.

Cover Design by Kim Russell / Wahoo Designs
Page Layout by Bart Dawson

ISBN 1-58334-369-5

ABOVE ALL ELSE
Directions for life

MEN

Above all else, guard your heart, for it
affects everything you do.
Proverbs 4:23-27 NLT

TABLE OF CONTENTS

Above all else, guard your heart, for it affects everything you do. Avoid all perverse talk; stay far from corrupt speech. Look straight ahead, and fix your eyes on what lies before you. Mark out a straight path for your feet; then stick to the path and stay safe. Don't get sidetracked; keep your feet from following evil.

Proverbs 4:23-27 NLT

ABOVE ALL ELSE . . .

A PARABLE BY TIM WAY

To the casual observer, the old man might have appeared to be dead. He had sat slumped in the large chair for the past three hours—his chin resting on his chest, eyes closed. Every now and then, his eyelids would twitch, or a soft sigh would escape his throat, but other than that, he was perfectly still. An undignified stream of drool had slowly rolled from one corner of his mouth and run into his white beard.

King Solomon was asleep.

The harsh sound of pottery smashing against a wall suddenly interrupted his peace. It was not close, mind you, but close enough to filter into his subconscious and bring him into that foggy place between sleep and wakefulness. For several minutes, he drifted back and forth.

When he'd earlier let weariness overtake him, it was just after noon. Now through half-closed eyelids, he could see that the late afternoon sun pierced through the western windows of the large study at a sharp angle, sending shafts of light through the latticework in the two narrow openings. The brightness made bold geometric patterns on the floor. He sat for some time contemplating the flecks of dust floating in the hazy glow, watching the patterns of light in their almost imperceptible march across the room.

He raised his head. "I love this place," he thought as he looked around. Of all the private rooms in his palace, this study was his favorite—a place he visited often. Now in the later part of his reign, he came here almost daily. Some days he came to escape the grueling pace of palace life, some days to write, and some days just to think or take a nap. Most would consider this sitting and watching and thinking a waste of time, but he did not. Sitting, watching, and thinking had been the genesis of numerous revelations.

"What woke me?" he muttered. "No, not you," he said as he looked down at the large, sleeping dog whose gray muzzle rested on his feet. No one else in his kingdom dared assume such an intimate closeness. "You're almost as ancient as me, old girl," the old king chuckled as he reached to scratch the dog's shaggy head.

Then he heard it again—crashing pottery followed by angry voices coming from the women's chambers. He moaned. "Not again. Why can't they get along? I should have stopped with only one. What made me think that seven hundred wives could exist peacefully with each other? They are like the constant dripping of water, wearing me down little by little. And there are hundreds of them, always nagging, whining, shouting and yapping like a bunch of spoiled children from sunup to sundown."

He put his head in his hands and sighed deeply.

While he only kept fifty or so of his most favored wives at the main palace, even that was no guarantee that they would not become violent with each other. Some did not even speak his language, and some he had only seen on their wedding day. Most of them he had married as a part of what he considered the cost of keeping peace with his neighbors. "And they are quite a cost," he thought. "They have cost me peace of mind and a part of my soul." He was so much closer to Yahweh before all of this marrying and accumulation of wealth.

The king's study was a perfect square—the top story of a tower sitting in the middle of the palace wall, extending four stories up from the ground. The tower's western wall formed a part of the outer wall of the palace. There were windows on all sides—two on each wall. The eastern windows overlooked a large courtyard in the interior of the palace. The courtyard, over three hundred square feet, was surrounded on three sides by the palace's interior buildings, and on the west by the outer wall and the tower. The western windows looked out over one of the busiest streets in Jerusalem. Here, people moved about in their daily routines, unaware that they were often being observed by the king. The north and south windows of the tower room looked down each length of the western palace wall. To the south, he could see the walls of the great temple with the Holy Place extending toward the heavens. The walls of the Holy Place were trimmed in pure gold and gleamed in the setting spring sun. Of all his accomplishments, the Temple of Yahweh was his most prized.

Two of his soldiers could be seen moving along the palace wall on patrol. They were dressed in the crisp blue and white dress uniform of the palace guard. Each carried a polished bronze shield that was a replica of the pure gold shields hanging in the great ceremonial hall, and their spears were tipped with genuine silver. His soldiers were not there because of any known threats to the kingdom, but because prudence demanded that they remain on guard. Besides, the palace walls were three stories high and the entire complex stood as a virtual fortress in the middle of one of the most fortified cities in the world.

The study's stone walls were lined with fragrant cedar from Lebanon. Even though the paneling had been installed fifteen years prior, it still had a sweet fragrance that greeted visitors to the room. Tapestries of incomparable value hung over the paneling—gifts from kings in surrounding countries. The furniture was heavy and finely carved, most of it built for appearance rather than comfort. But the chair in which the king sat was designed specifically for his rather stout frame. Its perfect fit and thick padding, along with a built-in footrest made this the perfect place for thinking—and sleeping.

The room was not originally intended to be a private

study. It was actually built as a part of the defensive aspects of the palace, but because of the extended peace, it was not needed for that purpose. So, the king had long ago claimed it as his personal study—a private sanctuary and his place to write letters, proverbs and poetry. The perfect view of the city and the temple, and the solitude it provided, made this simple room the king's most favorite spot on earth.

Solomon sat for another twenty minutes watching the sun's slow march across the stone floor. It was approaching twilight. Reaching for the wine goblet, he snorted in frustration when he found it empty. He was about to ring the bell to summon a servant when he heard voices filtering up from the street below.

"Here they are again," he said to the dog. Grunting loudly, he pulled himself up out of the chair and shuffled across to the window, the dog following closely but lazily at his heels.

Looking down through the ornate lattice work to the street below, he watched a group of young men in their late teens standing together. They were noisy and brash with a cockiness that came from inexperience and youth. Their voices were far too loud, and even though it was early evening, they were well on their way to being drunk. Their bragging about yet unaccomplished exploits only enhanced their foolishness. If they were trying to impress the palace guards looking down from the wall, they were wasting their time. Real men like his soldiers were only mildly amused by boys pretending to be men.

He had observed them here before. They frequented a tavern two streets over, and were just beginning to discover the joys of wasting their fathers' money on wine and who knows what all else.

The king shook his head. "If only they realized how utterly foolish they sound!" He was glad that his son, Rehoboam, was not a part of this group. "But only because I won't let him. If I gave him half a chance he would be down there with them. No, on second thought, he would be down there leading them in their folly," he thought.

The group began to move up the street to his right. One young man, however, hung back. "Hey, Judah, are you coming with us?" they called out to him.

"Uh, no. Not right now. You go on ahead. Maybe I'll catch up later. The usual place?" Judah replied, glancing over his shoulder as he spoke.

"Okay. Sure. Your loss!" they shouted back as they walked away.

"Maybe there is hope for this one," the old king thought. But then he looked up the street to his left and saw her. She was slowly pacing back and forth at the head of the lane. He had seen her before. She was in her late twenties; the only wife of an old wealthy merchant who often left Jerusalem to travel to Lebanon and beyond in search of wares to sell in his shop. She had married him not for love, but for his money. Now, as she often did when left by herself, she had painted her face and had traded her everyday clothes for a costume more suited to her true nature. Her clothes were clearly intended to attract the men that visited this street in search for a companion for the night—for a price. Here, on the other side of the city from her home, she could pretend to be someone else, luring men into a squalid rented room that she paid for from the profits of her part-time trade.

What motivated her to act like a prostitute? Was it the money? Not likely. Her husband gave her anything she wanted. Was it the excitement or the need to feel desired? No one aside from her and Yahweh would ever know.

The young man had seen this woman standing on this corner before and had determined that he would one day work up enough courage to approach her. For a price, he knew that he could have her for the evening, even though under normal circumstances, she would not give his young face a second glance.

She stood with her hands on her hips, watching him approach. His steps were a little unsteady, betraying his inability to handle his wine. He was trying his best to act nonchalant, but was unsuccessful in the attempt. Glancing nervously this way and that, he was obviously trying to assure that his father or one of his father's associates was not watching. When he was about five feet away from her, she shocked him by running up, boldly taking his face in her hands, and kissing him full on the mouth.

"Stop!" the king cried out. "You fool!" For a moment Judah hesitated. What was that he had just heard? He looked nervously behind him. Seeing no one, he gave his attention back to the woman.

She threw her head back and laughed loudly. "Come with me, my love. I have the makings of a feast—today I made my offerings, my vows are all paid!" The sound of her voice carried from the street up to the tower window.

"This woman is fit only for stoning," the king muttered to himself. "Moses and my father David would not have put up with this foolishness. Why have we gone so far astray from the ancient ways? The very nerve this woman has—to bring the things of God into this sinful act!"

The young man looked frantically around him. He had not expected her to be so bold or so loud. He was beginning to regret his decision. Besides, she did not look as good up close as she did from the other end of the street, and her breath smelled of stale wine.

"So now I've come to find you, hoping to catch sight of your face—and here you are!" she continued loudly.

"You liar!" thought the king. "You would have latched onto the first idiot that came down the street with money in his pocket."

Putting her arms around the young man and pulling him close, she purred, "Come, my love. I've spread fresh, clean sheets on my bed, colorful imported linens. My bed is covered with spices and exotic fragrances. Come! Let's make love all night and spend the night in ecstatic lovemaking! My husband's not home. He's away on business and he won't be back for a month."

With that, she put her arm through the young man's, and steered him down the street like a sheep going to slaughter, laughing loudly as she led him out of sight.

"If her husband finds out who has been sleeping with her while he is gone, he will have one of his servants cut out this young fool's heart and throw it to his dogs," the king thought. He was suddenly overcome with a great sadness—for the young man and for all of the young men in his nation. "Why, oh why, my Lord, do they behave so foolishly? Why do they act in this manner?"

While he hadn't actually expected an answer, one came clearly and immediately. The sudden impact almost drove him to his knees.

"It is because they have such poor example as a king," the Spirit spoke. "It is because the spiritual fervor has left your kingdom and has been replaced by a shallow, token nod to me, Yahweh, in the midst of obscene materialism. I have blessed you, but you have squandered my blessings by forgetting me!"

Solomon slowly sank into the chair at the desk. Holding his head in his hands, he slowly rocked back and forth as he let the words from the Spirit sink deep into his soul. His mind drifted back over the years of his reign. What promise! What blessings! Now, nothing was left but regrets and broken potential. He had more wealth than he could count, yet he was miserable. His people were wandering further and further away from Yahweh. How could so much be right, and yet everything be so wrong? Oh, for the smile of Yahweh once again!

Solomon sighed as he picked up the quill lying on the desk and dipped it in the inkwell. It had been a long time since he had felt the Spirit stirring in him. Years of self indulgence had dulled the moving of Yahweh on his soul, and the occurrences of divine inspiration on his writing had all but stopped. Today, however, was different. The Spirit's moving had started long before dawn and had continued into the noon hour. The words seemed to spill out of him onto the parchment. It was like years ago, when he regularly felt Yahweh's tug on his heart.

He looked at the last words he had written in the hours before his nap. His thoughts were of his son, Rehoboam, the one that would likely inherit the kingdom. "The boy is brash and foolish," he thought. "He speaks without thinking. Without my strong hand on his backside he would be out on the street with those other drunken fools. He listens to no one but the young men that surround him—young pups of privilege who are totally out of touch with the people. How will he govern a people he does not even understand or care about? Oh, if only he were more like his grandfather, David. I fear for the people of Israel when I go to be with my fathers."

Early that morning, Solomon had walked up the flight of stairs to the tower room and sat in this very spot watching the sun rise over the palace buildings. The Spirit had stirred deeply on his soul and he had written, *"The path of the righteous is like the first gleam of dawn, shining ever brighter till the full light of day. But the way of the wicked is like deep darkness; they do not know what makes them stumble."*

His thoughts went back to the young man on the street. "This could apply fully to him," the king thought. "He is stumbling around in the dark and will end up in a hole that will destroy him."

His thoughts went to his own son. As he began to write, he could feel the stirring once again of the Spirit and his pen moved urgently across the parchment.

"My son, pay attention to what I say; listen closely to my words. Do not let them out of your sight, keep them within your heart; for they are life to those who find them and health to a man's whole body."

Where had he gone wrong? What were the early signs that he was going the wrong direction? His heart had once burned hot for Jehovah. He thought back to the dedication of the temple and that awesome time when the presence of God filled the Holy of Holies on that dedication day. What an experience!

Then there was God's promise to bless him when he chose wisdom over riches. And the blessings that had poured in on him were more than he could have ever imagined in his wildest dreams. He had riches, power, wisdom—success at every turn.

But something happened. Maybe it was the great success. Maybe it was the ease with which wealth came his way. Maybe it was the many wives. He could justify them by saying they were necessary to make alliances, but the fact was that Jehovah had said not to take many wives. The end result was that his heart had grown cold—almost dead.

So, he threw himself into every pursuit he could imagine; intellectual pursuits, money, power, science, and building projects. None of them brought any satisfaction. All of it was pure vanity.

He turned his eyes back to the parchment in front of him. The Spirit's warmth washed over his body, and almost as if his hand took on a life of its own, he wrote again.

"Above all else, guard your heart, for it is the wellspring of life."

"That's it!" he almost shouted. "I have let down my guard and deceived my heart."

"What should I have done, my Lord?" he whispered. The Spirit whispered back the answer softly through his soul. Tears began to course down his wrinkled face, as his quill touched the paper once again.

"Put away perversity from your mouth; keep corrupt talk far from your lips. Let your eyes look straight ahead, fix your gaze directly before you. Make level paths for your feet and take only ways that are firm. Do not swerve to the right or the left; keep your foot from evil."

Through his tears, the old king looked at what he had just written. "My God, I repent before you," he said as he fell to his old knees and wept. "I will take a spotless lamb to your temple when the sun rises in the morning, and make a proper sacrifice for my sins. Forgive me, Yahweh, for letting down the guard on my heart, for speaking in ways that displease you, for looking and coveting what was not really mine to own, and most of all, for taking paths that were not firm. It is too late for me. I have been a poor example to my sons and my nation. I fear the price they will pay for my sins. Be gracious to them, my God."

The sun had set and darkness had settled over the palace when the old king finally rose slowly and stiffly to his feet. He rang the bell for his servant. He would have something sent up from the kitchen to eat. Something simple.

Even though nothing had really changed, he suddenly felt lighter. Though the urging of the Spirit had lifted, he knew that he had probably just written the most important words of his life. He would give them to his son. Would he listen? Probably not, but he would try anyway.

If not Rehoboam, then perhaps someone else in the future would benefit from the words given to him that day by Jehovah.

My son, pay attention to what I say; listen closely to my
*   words.*
Do not let them out of your sight, keep them within your heart;
For they are life to those who find them
And health to a man's whole body.
Above all else, guard your heart, for it is the wellspring of life.
Put away perversity from your mouth; keep corrupt talk far
*   from your lips.*
Let your eyes look straight ahead, fix your gaze directly before
*   you.*
Make level paths for your feet and take only ways that are
*   firm.*
Do not swerve to the right or the left; keep your foot from evil.

Proverbs 4:20–27

While the scene of the young man and the prostitute is fictional, it has basis in fact and can be found in Proverbs 7:6–23.

INTRODUCTION

God's Word is clear: we are to guard our hearts "above all else," yet we live in a world that encourages us to do otherwise. Here in the 21st century, temptations and distractions are woven into the fabric of everyday life. As believers, we must remain vigilant. Not only must we resist Satan when he confronts us, but we must also avoid those places where Satan can most easily tempt us. And, this book is intended to help.

In Proverbs 4:23-27, we are instructed to guard our words, our eyes, and our path. This text examines these instructions through a collection of essays, Bible verses, and quotations from noted Christian thinkers.

As a way of introducing these ideas, this book begins with a parable by Tim Way—a story about temptation in the ancient city Jerusalem and about how human waywardness, coupled with divine insight, might have influenced the writings of an aged king. Tim's story is followed by a series of practical lessons, lessons about protecting ourselves against the trials and temptations that have become inescapable elements of modern-day life.

Each day, you must make countless choices that can bring you closer to God, or not. When you guard your heart—and when you live in accordance with God's commandments—you will inevitably earn His blessings. But if you make unwise choices, or if you yield to the temptations of this difficult age, you must pay a price for your shortsightedness, perhaps a very high price.

Would you like to avoid the dangers and temptations that Satan will inevitably place along your path? And would you like to experience God's peace and His abundance? Then guard your heart above all else. When you're tempted to speak an unkind word, hold your tongue. When you're faced with a difficult choice or a powerful temptation, seek God's counsel and trust the counsel He gives. When you're uncertain of your next step, follow in the footsteps of God's only begotten Son. Invite God into your heart and live according to His commandments. When you do, you will be blessed today, tomorrow, and forever.

PART 1

GUARD
YOUR WORDS

Avoid all perverse talk;
stay far from corrupt speech.
Proverbs 4:24 NLT

GUARD
YOUR SPEECH

Pleasant words are a honeycomb:
sweet to the taste and health to the body.

Proverbs 16:24 Holman CSB

Think . . . pause . . . then speak: How wise is the man who can communicate in this way. But all too often, in the rush to have ourselves heard, we speak first and think next . . . with unfortunate results.

God's Word reminds us that "Reckless words pierce like a sword, but the tongue of the wise brings healing" (Proverbs 12:18 NIV). If we seek to be a source of encouragement to friends and family, then we must measure our words carefully. Words are important: they can hurt or heal. Words can uplift us or discourage us, and reckless words, spoken in haste, cannot be erased.

Today, seek to encourage all who cross your path. Measure your words carefully. Speak wisely, not impulsively. Use words of kindness and praise, not words of anger or derision. Remember that you have the power to heal others or to injure them, to lift others up or to hold them back. When you lift them up, your wisdom will bring healing and comfort to a world that needs both.

Avoid all perverse talk;
stay far from corrupt speech.

Proverbs 4:24 NLT

A TIP FOR GUARDING YOUR HEART

Words, words, words . . . are important, important, important! So make sure that you think first and speak next. Otherwise, you may give the greatest speech you wish you'd never made!

WORDS OF WISDOM

Happy is the man whose words issue from the Holy Spirit and not from himself.

Anthony of Padua

In all your deeds and words, you should look on Jesus as your model, whether you are keeping silence or speaking, whether you are alone or with others.

St. Bonaventure

There is nothing more similar to a wise man than a fool who keeps quiet.

St. Francis of Sales

Change the heart, and you change the speech.

Warren Wiersbe

Every word we speak, every action we take, has an effect on the totality of humanity. No one can escape that privilege—or that responsibility.

Laurie Beth Jones

GOD'S WORDS OF WISDOM

For the one who wants to love life and to see good days must keep his tongue from evil and his lips from speaking deceit.

1 Peter 3:10 Holman CSB

Avoid irreverent, empty speech, for this will produce an even greater measure of godlessness.

2 Timothy 2:16 Holman CSB

No rotten talk should come from your mouth, but only what is good for the building up of someone in need, in order to give grace to those who hear.

Ephesians 4:29 Holman CSB

If anyone thinks he is religious, without controlling his tongue but deceiving his heart, his religion is useless.

James 1:26 Holman CSB

SUMMING IT UP

God understands the importance of the words you speak . . . and so must you.

GUARD YOUR WORDS WITH INTEGRITY

The integrity of the upright will guide them.

Proverbs 11:3 NKJV

Charles Swindoll correctly observed, "Nothing speaks louder or more powerfully than a life of integrity." Godly men and women agree.

Integrity is built slowly over a lifetime. It is the sum of every right decision and every honest word. It is forged on the anvil of honorable work and polished by the twin virtues of honesty and fairness. Integrity is a precious thing—difficult to build but easy to tear down.

As believers in Christ, we must seek to live each day with discipline, honesty, and faith. When we do, at least two things happen: integrity becomes a habit, and God blesses us because of our obedience to Him.

Living a life of integrity isn't always the easiest way, but it is always the right way. God clearly intends that it should be our way, too.

Oswald Chambers advised, "Never support an experience which does not have God as its source, and faith in God as its result." These words serve as a powerful reminder that, as Christians, we are called to walk with God and obey His commandments. But, we live in a world that presents us with countless temptations to stray far from God's path. We Christians, when confronted with sins of any kind, have clear instructions: Walk—or better yet run—in the opposite direction.

It has been said that character is what we are when nobody is watching. How true. When we do things that we know aren't right, we try to hide them from our families and friends. But even if we successfully conceal our sins from the world, we can never conceal our sins from God.

If you sincerely wish to walk with your Creator, follow His commandments. When you do, your character will take care of itself . . . and you won't need to look over your shoulder to see who, besides God, is watching.

A TIP FOR GUARDING YOUR HEART

Remember: Character is more important than popularity.

WORDS OF WISDOM

The trials of life can be God's tools for engraving His image on our character.

Warren Wiersbe

This world is not our home, and we lament its sin-wrecked condition, riddled with disease and death and distress. But, for the growing of Christian character, it is a proper training ground.

Vance Havner

In matters of style, swim with the current. In matters of principle, stand like a rock.

Thomas Jefferson

Character is both developed and revealed by tests, and all of life is a test.

Rick Warren

Character is made in the small moments of our lives.

Phillips Brooks

GOD'S WORDS OF WISDOM

The man of integrity walks securely, but he who takes crooked paths will be found out.

Proverbs 10:9 NIV

A good name is more desirable than great riches; to be esteemed is better than silver or gold.

Proverbs 22:1 NIV

As in water face reflects face, so the heart of man reflects man.

Proverbs 27:19 NASB

Not only so, but we also rejoice in our sufferings, because we know that suffering produces perseverance; perseverance, character; and character, hope.

Romans 5:3-4 NIV

SUMMING IT UP

When your words are honest and your intentions are pure, you have nothing to fear. Thus, you should guard your integrity even more carefully than you guard your wallet.

GUARD YOUR WORDS AGAINST ANGER

An angry man stirs up dissension,
and a hot-tempered one commits many sins.

Proverbs 29:22 NIV

If you're like most men, you know a thing or two about anger. After all, everybody gets mad occasionally, and you're no exception.

Anger is a natural human emotion that is sometimes necessary and appropriate. Even Jesus became angry when confronted with the moneychangers in the temple: "And Jesus entered the temple and drove out all those who were buying and selling in the temple, and overturned the tables of the moneychangers and the seats of those who were selling doves" (Matthew 21:12 NASB).

Righteous indignation is an appropriate response to evil, but God does not intend that anger should rule our lives. Far from it. God intends that we turn away from anger whenever possible and forgive our neighbors just as we seek forgiveness for ourselves.

Life is full of frustrations: some great and some small. On occasion, you, like Jesus, will confront evil, and when you do, you may respond as He did: vigorously and without reservation. But, more often your frustrations will be of the more mundane variety. As long as you live here on earth, you will face countless opportunities to lose your temper over small, relatively insignificant events: a traffic jam, an inconsiderate comment, or a broken promise. When you are tempted to lose your temper over the minor inconveniences of life, don't. Instead of turning up the heat, walk away. Turn away from anger, hatred, bitterness, and regret. Turn, instead, to God. When you do, you'll be following His commandments and giving yourself a priceless gift . . . the gift of peace.

A Tip for Guarding Your Heart

Write a scouting report for your tantrums: If you'd like to defeat temper tantrums before they start—which, by the way, is the best time to defeat them—try writing down a detailed scouting report of the people and situations that cause you to go off. Then write down better, more productive ways to deal with your problems. The best time to tackle trouble is before it gets rolling, not after . . . and the same can be said of your anger. So think ahead and plan ahead.

WORDS OF WISDOM

Anger breeds remorse in the heart, discord in the home,
bitterness in the community, and confusion in the state.

Billy Graham

Get rid of the poison of built-up anger and the acid of
long-term resentment.

Charles Swindoll

When you strike out in anger, you may miss the other
person, but you will always hit yourself.

Jim Gallery

Anger is the noise of the soul; the unseen irritant of the
heart; the relentless invader of silence.

Max Lucado

Take no action in a furious passion. It's putting to sea in a
storm.

Thomas Fuller

GOD'S WORDS OF WISDOM

And the servant of the Lord must not strive; but be gentle unto all men, apt to teach, patient; in meekness instructing those that oppose themselves . . . .

2 Timothy 2:24-25 KJV

A patient man has great understanding, but a quick-tempered man displays folly.

Proverbs 14:29 NIV

But I tell you that men will have to give account on the day of judgment for every careless word they have spoken. For by your words you will be acquitted, and by your words you will be condemned.

Matthew 12:36-37 NIV

SUMMING IT UP

Angry words are dangerous to your emotional and spiritual health, not to mention your relationships. So treat anger as an uninvited guest, and usher it away as quickly—and as quietly—as possible.

GUARD YOUR WORDS BY REMAINING HUMBLE

Therefore humble yourselves under the mighty hand of God,
that He may exalt you in due time,
casting all your care upon Him, for He cares for you.
1 Peter 5:6-7 NKJV

Humility is not, in most cases, a naturally occurring human trait. Most of us, it seems, are more than willing to overestimate our own accomplishments. We are tempted to say, "Look how wonderful I am!" . . . hoping all the while that the world will agree with our own self-appraisals. But those of us who fall prey to the sin of pride should beware—God is definitely not impressed by our prideful proclamations.

God honors humility . . . and He rewards those who humbly serve Him. So if you've acquired the wisdom to be humble, then you are to be congratulated. But if you've not yet overcome the tendency to overestimate your own accomplishments, then God still has some important (and perhaps painful) lessons to teach you—lessons about humility that you still need to learn.

You will save the humble people;
But Your eyes are on the haughty,
that You may bring them down.

2 Samuel 22:28 NKJV

A TIP FOR GUARDING YOUR HEART

Do you value humility above status? If so, God will smile upon your endeavors. But if you value status above humility, you're inviting God's displeasure. In short, humility pleases God; pride does not.

WORDS OF WISDOM

Jesus had a humble heart. If He abides in us, pride will never dominate our lives.

Billy Graham

Humility is the fairest and rarest flower that blooms.

Charles Swindoll

Let the love of Christ be believed in and felt in your hearts, and it will humble you.

C. H. Spurgeon

Humility expresses a genuine dependency on God and others.

Charles Stanley

Humility is an attitude. The Lord is high and lifted up, and we are supposed to take a position of lowliness.

Franklin Graham

GOD'S WORDS OF WISDOM

Finally, all of you should be of one mind, full of sympathy toward each other, loving one another with tender hearts and humble minds.

1 Peter 3:8 NLT

God is against the proud, but he gives grace to the humble.

1 Peter 5:5 NCV

If My people who are called by My name will humble themselves, and pray and seek My face, and turn from their wicked ways, then I will hear from heaven, and will forgive their sin and heal their land.

2 Chronicles 7:14 NKJV

Do nothing out of rivalry or conceit, but in humility consider others as more important than yourselves.

Philippians 2:3 Holman CSB

SUMMING IT UP

You must remain humble or face the consequences. Pride does go before the fall, but humility often prevents the fall.

GUARD YOUR WORDS AGAINST BITTERNESS

*Get rid of all bitterness, rage, anger, harsh words,
and slander, as well as all types of malicious behavior.
Instead, be kind to each other, tenderhearted,
forgiving one another, just as God
through Christ has forgiven you.*

Ephesians 4:31-32 NLT

It has been said that life is an exercise in forgiveness. How true. Christ understood the importance of forgiveness when He commanded, "Love your enemies and pray for those who persecute you" (Matthew 5:44 NIV). But sometimes, forgiveness is difficult indeed.

When we have been injured or embarrassed, we feel the urge to strike back and to hurt the one who has hurt us. Christ instructs us to do otherwise. Believers are taught that forgiveness is God's way and that mercy is an integral part of God's plan for our lives. In short, we are commanded to weave the thread of forgiveness into the very fabric of our lives.

Today, as you go about your daily affairs, remember that you have already been forgiven by your Heavenly Father, and so, too, should you forgive others. If you bear bitterness against anyone, take your bitterness to God and leave it there. If you are angry, pray for God's healing hand to calm your spirit. If you are troubled by some past injustice, read God's Word and remember His commandment to forgive. When you follow that commandment and sincerely forgive those who have hurt you, you'll discover that a heavy burden has been lifted from your shoulders. And, you'll discover that although forgiveness is indeed difficult, with God's help, all things are possible.

> *Hatred stirs up trouble,*
> *but love forgives all wrongs.*
>
> Proverbs 10:12 NCV

A TIP FOR GUARDING YOUR HEART

Today, think about the people you still need to forgive. And then ask God to help you forgive them.

WORDS OF WISDOM

Revenge is the raging fire that consumes the arsonist.

Max Lucado

To hold on to hate and resentments is to throw a monkey wrench into the machinery of life.

E. Stanley Jones

Our forgiveness toward others should flow from a realization and appreciation of God's forgiveness toward us.

Franklin Graham

By not forgiving, by not letting wrongs go, we aren't getting back at anyone. We are merely punishing ourselves by barricading our own hearts.

Jim Cymbala

I firmly believe a great many prayers are not answered because we are not willing to forgive someone.

D. L. Moody

GOD'S WORDS OF WISDOM

Be even-tempered, content with second place, quick to forgive an offense. Forgive as quickly and completely as the Master forgave you. And regardless of what else you put on, wear love. It's your basic, all-purpose garment. Never be without it.

Colossians 3:13-14 MSG

Have mercy on me, O God, according to your unfailing love; according to your great compassion blot out my transgressions. Wash away all my iniquity and cleanse me from my sin.

Psalm 51:1-2 NIV

If you forgive those who sin against you, your heavenly Father will forgive you. But if you refuse to forgive others, your Father will not forgive your sins.

Matthew 6:14-15 NLT

SUMMING IT UP

Forgiveness is its own reward. Bitterness is its own punishment. Guard your words and your thoughts accordingly.

GUARD YOUR WORDS AGAINST THE TEMPTATION TO JUDGE

Do not judge, and you will not be judged.
Do not condemn, and you will not be condemned.
Forgive, and you will be forgiven.

Luke 6:37 Holman CSB

E ven the most devoted Christians may fall prey to a powerful yet subtle temptation: the temptation to judge others. But as believers, we are commanded to refrain from such behavior. The warning of Matthew 7:1 is clear: "Judge not, that ye be not judged" (KJV).

Are you one of those people who finds it easy to judge others? If so, it's time to make radical changes in the way you view the world and the people who inhabit it.

When considering the shortcomings of others, you must remember this: in matters of judgment, God does not need (or want) your help. Why? Because God is perfectly capable of judging the human heart . . . while you are not. This message is made clear by the teachings of Jesus.

As Jesus came upon a young woman who had been condemned by the Pharisees, He spoke not only to the crowd that was gathered there, but also to all generations, when He warned, "He that is without sin among you, let him first cast a stone at her" (John 8:7 KJV). Christ's message is clear: because we are all sinners, we are commanded to refrain from judging others. Yet the irony is this: it is precisely because we are sinners that we are so quick to judge.

All of us have all fallen short of God's laws, and none of us, therefore, are qualified to "cast the first stone." Thankfully, God has forgiven us, and we, too, must forgive others. Let us refrain, then, from judging our family members, our friends, and our loved ones. Instead, let us forgive them and love them in the same way that God has forgiven us.

A TIP FOR GUARDING YOUR HEART

When you catch yourself being overly judgmental, try to stop yourself and interrupt your critical thoughts before you become angry.

WORDS OF WISDOM

An individual Christian may see fit to give up all sorts of things for special reasons—marriage, or meat, or beer, or cinema; but the moment he starts saying these things are bad in themselves, or looking down his nose at other people who do use them, he has taken the wrong turn.

C. S. Lewis

Forget the faults of others by remembering your own.

John Bunyan

No creed or school of thought can monopolize the Spirit of God.

Oswald Chambers

Turn your attention upon yourself and beware of judging the deeds of other men, for in judging others a man labors vainly, often makes mistakes, and easily sins; whereas, in judging and taking stock of himself he does something that is always profitable.

Thomas à Kempis

Being critical of others, including God, is one way we try to avoid facing and judging our own sins.

Warren Wiersbe

GOD'S WORDS OF WISDOM

You, therefore, have no excuse, you who pass judgment on someone else, for at whatever point you judge the other, you are condemning yourself.

Romans 2:1 NIV

Speak and act as those who will be judged by the law of freedom. For judgment is without mercy to the one who hasn't shown mercy. Mercy triumphs over judgment.

James 2:12-13 Holman CSB

Therefore judge nothing before the time, until the Lord comes, who will both bring to light the hidden things of darkness and reveal the counsels of the hearts. Then each one's praise will come from God.

1 Corinthians 4:5 NKJV

SUMMING IT UP

To the extent you judge others, so, too, will you be judged. So you must, to the best of your ability, refrain from judgmental thoughts and words.

GUARD YOUR WORDS BY STRIVING TO BE PATIENT

Always be humble, gentle, and patient,
accepting each other in love.

Ephesians 4:2 NCV

Are you a man in a hurry? If so, you're probably not the only one in your neighborhood. We human beings are, by our very nature, impatient. We are impatient with others, impatient with ourselves, and impatient with our Creator. We want things to happen according to our own timetables, but our Heavenly Father may have other plans. That's why we must learn the art of patience.

All too often, we are unwilling to trust God's perfect timing. We allow ourselves to become apprehensive and anxious as we wait nervously for God to act. Usually, we know what we want, and we know precisely when we want it: right now, if not sooner. But, when God's plans differ from our own, we must train ourselves to trust in His infinite wisdom and in His infinite love.

As people living in a fast-paced world, many of us find that waiting quietly for God is quite troubling. But in our better moments, we realize that patience is not only a virtue, but it is also a commandment from the Creator.

Psalm 37:7 makes it clear that we should "Be still before the Lord and wait patiently for Him" (NIV). But ours is a generation that usually places little value on stillness and patience. No matter. God instructs us to be patient in all things, and we must obey Him or suffer the consequences of His displeasure.

We must be patient with our families, with our friends, and with ourselves. We must also be patient with our Heavenly Father as He shapes our world (and our lives) in accordance with His timetable, not our own. And that's as it should be. After all, think how patient God has been with us.

A TIP FOR GUARDING YOUR HEART

If you want folks to be patient with you, then you must do the same for them. Never expect other people to be more patient with you than you are with them.

WORDS OF WISDOM

You can't step in front of God and not get in trouble.
When He says, "Go three steps," don't go four.

Charles Stanley

God is more patient with us than we are with ourselves.

Max Lucado

If God is diligent, surely we ought to be diligent in doing
our duty to Him. Think how patient and diligent God has
been to us!

Oswald Chambers

In all negotiations of difficulties, a man may not look to
sow and reap at once. He must prepare his business and so
ripen it by degrees.

Francis Bacon

In the Bible, patience is not a passive acceptance of
circumstances. It is a courageous perseverance in the face
of suffering and difficulty.

Warren Wiersbe

GOD'S WORDS OF WISDOM

Patience is better than strength.

Proverbs 16:32 NCV

Patience and encouragement come from God. And I pray that God will help you all agree with each other the way Christ Jesus wants.

Romans 15:5 NCV

But if we look forward to something we don't have yet, we must wait patiently and confidently.

Romans 8:25 NLT

The Lord is wonderfully good to those who wait for him and seek him. So it is good to wait quietly for salvation from the Lord.

Lamentations 3:25-26 NLT

SUMMING IT UP

When you learn to be more patient with others, you'll make your world—and your heart—a better place.

GUARD YOUR WORDS WITH CONSTANT PRAISE FOR THE CREATOR

Praise the Lord! Oh, give thanks to the Lord, for He is good!
For His mercy endures forever.

Psalm 106:1 NKJV

If you'd like to guard your heart and strengthen your character, try spending more time praising God. When, by the way, is the best time to praise God? In church? Before dinner is served? When we tuck little children into bed? None of the above. The best time to praise God is all day, every day, to the greatest extent we can, with thanksgiving in our hearts.

Too many of us, even well-intentioned believers, tend to "compartmentalize" our waking hours into a few familiar categories: work, rest, play, family time, and worship. To do so is a mistake. Worship and praise should be woven into the fabric of everything we do; it should never be relegated to a weekly three-hour visit to church on Sunday morning.

Mrs. Charles E. Cowman, the author of the classic devotional text, *Streams in the Desert*, wrote, "Two wings are necessary to lift our souls toward God: prayer and praise. Prayer asks. Praise accepts the answer." Today, find a little more time to lift your concerns to God in prayer, and praise Him for all that He has done. He's listening . . . and He wants to hear from you.

> *The LORD is my strength and song,*
> *and He has become my salvation;*
> *He is my God, and I will praise Him.*
>
> *Exodus 15:2 NIV*

A TIP FOR GUARDING YOUR HEART

Remember that it always pays to praise your Creator. That's why thoughtful believers (like you) make it a habit to carve out quiet moments throughout the day to praise God.

WORDS OF WISDOM

The words "thank" and "think" come from the same root word. If we would think more, we would thank more.

Warren Wiersbe

A child of God should be a visible beatitude for joy and a living doxology for gratitude.

C. H. Spurgeon

Why wait until the fourth Thursday in November? Why wait until the morning of December twenty-fifth? Thanksgiving to God should be an everyday affair. The time to be thankful is now!

Jim Gallery

Praise reestablishes the proper chain of command; we recognize that the King is on the throne and that he has saved his people.

Max Lucado

It is only with gratitude that life becomes rich.

Dietrich Bonhoeffer

GOD'S WORDS OF WISDOM

Is anyone happy? Let him sing songs of praise.

James 5:13 NIV

Through Him then, let us continually offer up a sacrifice of praise to God, that is, the fruit of lips that give thanks to His name.

Hebrews 13:15 NASB

And suddenly there was with the angel a multitude of the heavenly host praising God and saying: "Glory to God in the highest, And on earth peace, goodwill toward men!"

Luke 2:13-14 NKJV

At the name of Jesus every knee should bow, of those in heaven, and of those on earth, and of those under the earth, and that every tongue should confess that Jesus Christ is Lord, to the glory of God the Father.

Philippians 2:10-11 NKJV

SUMMING IT UP

The appropriate moment to praise God is always this one.

GUARD YOUR WORDS AGAINST PROFANITY

Avoid all perverse talk; stay far from corrupt speech.

Proverbs 4:24 NLT

Modern society seems to have fallen in love with profanity. You hear offensive language everywhere: on the radio, in the movie theater, on television (especially cable TV!), and in most public places. It seems that inappropriate language has infiltrated our culture at almost every level. And that's unfortunate.

Just because society embraces profanity doesn't mean that you should embrace it, too. In fact, the opposite should be true: the more vulgar the world becomes, the more determined you should be to avoid using profanity. Why? Because that's what God wants you to do.

Throughout the Bible, God gives many warnings about the use of inappropriate language. And if you're wise, you'll take those warnings to heart even if lots of people don't.

So the next time you hear someone say something you wouldn't repeat in church, make sure that you don't join in. Profane words are against God's rules, and they should be against your rules, too.

Watch the way you talk.
Let nothing foul or dirty come out of your mouth.
Say only what helps, each word a gift.

Ephesians 4:29 MSG

A TIP FOR GUARDING YOUR HEART

You live in a society that, for the most part, condones profanity—but you must not.

WORDS OF WISDOM

Attitude and the spirit in which we communicate are as important as the words we say.

Charles Stanley

Perhaps we have been guilty of speaking against someone and have not realized how it may have hurt them. Then when someone speaks against us, we suddenly realize how deeply such words hurt, and we become sensitive to what we have done.

Theodore Epp

I still believe we ought to talk about Jesus. The old country doctor of my boyhood days always began his examination by saying, "Let me see your tongue." That's a good way to check a Christian: the tongue test. Let's hear what he is talking about.

Vance Havner

Like dynamite, God's power is only latent power until it is released. You can release God's dynamite power into people's lives and the world through faith, your words, and prayer.

Bill Bright

GOD'S WORDS OF WISDOM

So then, rid yourselves of all evil, all lying, hypocrisy, jealousy, and evil speech. As newborn babies want milk, you should want the pure and simple teaching. By it you can grow up and be saved.

1 Peter 2:1–2 NCV

Be gracious in your speech. The goal is to bring out the best in others in a conversation, not put them down, not cut them out.

Colossians 4:6 MSG

To everything there is a season . . . a time to keep silence, and a time to speak.

Ecclesiastes 3:1,7 KJV

SUMMING IT UP

Profanity has absolutely no place in your vocabulary. Period.

GUARD YOUR WORDS WITH SILENCE

Be silent before the Lord and wait expectantly for Him.

Psalm 37:7 Holman CSB

ere's a simple prescription for guarding your heart: carve out a little time for silence every day. Here in our noisy, 21st-century world, silence is highly underrated. Many of us can't even seem to walk from the front door to the street without a cell phone or an IPOD in our ear. The world seems to grow louder day by day, and our senses seem to be invaded at every turn. But, if we allow the distractions of a clamorous society to separate us from God's peace, we do ourselves a profound disservice. So if we're wise, we make time each day for quiet reflection. And when we do, we are rewarded.

Do you take time each day for an extended period of silence? And during those precious moments, do you sincerely open your heart to your Creator? If so, you will be blessed. If not, then the struggles and stresses of everyday living may rob you of the peace that should rightfully be yours because of your personal relationship with Christ. So take time each day to quietly commune with your Creator. When you do, those moments of silence will enable you to participate more fully in the only source of peace that endures: God's peace.

> ## The mightiest works of God are the fruit of silence.
>
> *F. B. Meyer*

A TIP FOR GUARDING YOUR HEART

Try this experiment: the next time you're driving alone in your automobile, do so without radio, CDs, or cell phones. And then, have a quiet talk with God about His plans for your life. You may be surprised to discover that sometimes the most important answers are the ones you receive in silence.

WORDS OF WISDOM

Silence is a gift of God, to let us speak more intimately with Him.

Vincent Pallotti

We know well enough how to keep outward silence, and to hush our spoken words, but we know little of interior silence. It consists in hushing our idle, restless, wandering imagination, in quieting the promptings of our worldly minds, and in suppressing the crowd of unprofitable thoughts which excite and disturb the soul.

François Fénelon

Growth takes place in quietness, in hidden ways, in silence and solitude. The process is not accessible to observation.

Eugene Peterson

Most of man's trouble comes from his inability to be still.

Blaise Pascal

GOD'S WORDS OF WISDOM

In quietness and trust is your strength.

Isaiah 30:15 NASB

Be still, and know that I am God.

Psalm 46:10 NKJV

I wait quietly before God, for my hope is in him.

Psalm 62:5 NLT

What's this? Fools out shopping for wisdom! They wouldn't recognize it if they saw it! One Who Knows Much Says Little.

Proverbs 17:16 MSG

Morning by morning he wakens me and opens my understanding to his will. The Sovereign Lord has spoken to me, and I have listened.

Isaiah 50:4-5 NLT

SUMMING IT UP

Spend a few moments each day in silence. You owe it to your Creator . . . and to yourself.

GUARD YOUR WORDS BY BEING KIND

Be kindly affectionate to one another with brotherly love,
in honor giving preference to one another; not lagging in
diligence, fervent in spirit, serving the Lord; rejoicing in hope,
patient in tribulation, continuing steadfastly in prayer.

Romans 12:10-12 NKJV

John Wesley's advice was straightforward: "Do all the good you can. By all the means you can. In all the ways you can. In all the places you can. At all the times you can. To all the people you can. As long as you can." One way to do all the good you can is to spread kindness wherever you go.

Sometimes, when we feel happy or generous, we find it easy to be kind. Other times, when we are discouraged or tired, we can scarcely summon the energy to utter a single kind word. But, God's commandment is clear: He intends that we make the conscious choice to treat others with kindness and respect, no matter our circumstances, no matter our emotions.

For Christians, kindness is not an option; it is a commandment. In the Gospel of Matthew, Jesus declares, "In everything, therefore, treat people the same way you want them to treat you, for this is the Law and the Prophets" (Matthew 7:12 NASB). Jesus did not say, "In some things, treat people as you wish to be treated." And, He did not say, "From time to time, treat others with kindness." Christ said that we should treat others as we wish to be treated "in everything." This, of course, is a difficult task, but as Christians, we are commanded to do our best.

Today, as you consider all the things that Christ has done in your life, honor Him by being a little kinder than necessary. Honor Him by slowing down long enough to offer encouragement to someone who needs it. Honor Him by picking up the phone and calling a distant friend . . . for no reason other than to say, "I'm thinking of you." Honor Christ with your good words and your good deeds. Jesus expects no less, and He deserves no less.

A TIP FOR GUARDING YOUR HEART

The Golden Rule starts with you, so when in doubt, be a little kinder than necessary.

WORDS OF WISDOM

If we have the true love of God in our hearts, we will show it in our lives. We will not have to go up and down the earth proclaiming it. We will show it in everything we say or do.

D. L. Moody

Scientists tell us that every word and picture ever broadcast electronically is still somewhere out in space, billions of miles away. If humans ever go to other planets, they may see an old episode of *Gunsmoke*. Amazing as that sounds, there is something even more astonishing: Not a single act of goodness in Jesus' name has ever disappeared. Every act of kindness reaches out and touches the lives of thousands of people—one at a time.

Dennis Swanberg

One of the greatest things a man can do for his Heavenly Father is to be kind to some of his other children.

Henry Drummond

While great brilliance and intellect are to be admired, they cannot dry one tear or mend a broken spirit. Only kindness can accomplish this.

John Drescher

GOD'S WORDS OF WISDOM

*Be kind to each other, tenderhearted, forgiving one another,
just as God through Christ has forgiven you.*

Ephesians 4:32 NLT

*Carry each other's burdens, and in this way you will fulfill the
law of Christ.*

Galatians 6:2 NIV

*Finally, all of you should be of one mind, full of sympathy
toward each other, loving one another with tender hearts and
humble minds.*

1 Peter 3:8 NLT

*And may the Lord make you increase and abound in love to
one another and to all.*

1 Thessalonians 3:12 NKJV

SUMMING IT UP

Kind words have echoes that last a lifetime and
beyond.

GUARD YOUR WORDS BY BEING GRATEFUL

Give thanks to the Lord, for He is good;
His faithful love endures forever.

Psalm 106:1 Holman CSB

God has blessed us beyond measure, and we owe Him everything, including our constant praise. That's why thanksgiving should become a habit, a regular part of our daily routines. When we slow down and express our gratitude to the One who made us, we enrich our own lives and the lives of those around us.

Dietrich Bonhoeffer observed, "It is only with gratitude that life becomes rich." These words most certainly apply to you.

As a follower of Christ, you have been blessed beyond measure. God sent His only Son to die for you. And, God has given you the priceless gifts of eternal love and eternal life. You, in turn, should approach your Heavenly Father with reverence and gratitude.

Are you a thankful person? Do you appreciate the gifts that God has given you? And, do you demonstrate your gratitude by being a faithful steward of the gifts and talents that you have received from your Creator? You most certainly should be thankful. After all, when you stop to think about it, God has given you more blessings than you can count. So the question of the day is this: will you thank your Heavenly Father . . . or will you spend your time and energy doing other things?

God is always listening—are you willing to say thanks? It's up to you, and the next move is yours.

Enter his gates with thanksgiving,
go into his courts with praise.
Give thanks to him and bless his name.

Psalm 100:4 NLT

A TIP FOR GUARDING YOUR HEART

By speaking words of thanksgiving and praise, you honor the Father and you protect your heart against the twin evils of apathy and ingratitude.

WORDS OF WISDOM

It is only with gratitude that life becomes rich.

Dietrich Bonhoeffer

A Christian who walks by faith accepts all circumstances from God. He thanks God when everything goes good, when everything goes bad, and for the "blues" somewhere in between. He thanks God whether he feels like it or not.

Erwin Lutzer

When it comes to life, the critical thing is whether you take things for granted or take them with gratitude.

G. K. Chesterton

The unthankful heart discovers no mercies; but the thankful heart will find, in every hour, some heavenly blessings!

Henry Ward Beecher

Grace and gratitude belong together like heaven and earth. Grace evokes gratitude like the voice of an echo. Gratitude follows grace as thunder follows lightning.

Karl Barth

GOD'S WORDS OF WISDOM

In everything give thanks; for this is the will of God in Christ Jesus for you.

1 Thessalonians 5:18 NKJV

My counsel for you is simple and straightforward: Just go ahead with what you've been given. You received Christ Jesus, the Master; now live him. You're deeply rooted in him. You're well constructed upon him. You know your way around the faith. Now do what you've been taught. School's out; quit studying the subject and start living it! And let your living spill over into thanksgiving.

Colossians 2:6-7 MSG

Finally, brethren, whatsoever things are true, whatsoever things are honest, whatsoever things are just, whatsoever things are pure, whatsoever things are lovely, whatsoever things are of good report; if there be any virtue, and if there be any praise, think on these things.

Philippians 4:8 KJV

SUMMING IT UP

You owe God everything . . . including your thanks.

PART 2

GUARD
YOUR EYES

Look straight ahead,
and fix your eyes on what lies before you.

Proverbs 4:25 NLT

GUARD YOUR EYES AGAINST THE WORLD'S MANY TEMPTATIONS

Look straight ahead, and fix your eyes on what lies before you.

Proverbs 4:25 NLT

It's inevitable: today you will be tempted by somebody or something—in fact, you will probably be tempted on countless occasions. Why? Because you live in a world that's filled to the brim with temptations and addictions that are intended to lead you far away from God.

Here in the 21st century, temptations are now completely and thoroughly woven into the fabric of everyday life. Seductive images are everywhere; subtle messages tell you that it's okay to sin "just a little"; and to make matters even worse, society doesn't just seem to endorse godlessness, it actually seems to reward it. Society spews forth a wide range of messages, all of which imply that it's okay to rebel against God. These messages, of course, are extremely dangerous and completely untrue.

How can you guard your heart against society's tidal wave of temptations? By learning to direct your thoughts and your eyes in ways that are pleasing to God . . . and by relying upon Him to deliver you from the evils that threaten you. And here's the good news: the Creator has promised (not implied, not suggested, not insinuated—He has promised!) that with His help, you can resist every single temptation that confronts you.

When it comes to fighting Satan, you are never alone. God is always with you, and if you do your part He will do His part. But what, precisely, is your part? A good starting point is simply learning how to recognize the subtle temptations that surround you. The images of immorality are ubiquitous, and they're intended to hijack your mind, your heart, your pocketbook, your life, and your soul. Don't let them do it.

Satan is both industrious and creative; he's working 24/7, and he's causing pain, heartache, trauma, and tragedy in more ways than ever before. You, as a Christian man of God, must remain watchful and strong—starting today and ending never.

A TIP FOR GUARDING YOUR HEART

You live in a society where temptations are everywhere. Your task is to avoid places where you might be tempted to disobey God.

WORDS OF WISDOM

The Bible teaches us in times of temptation there is one command: Flee! Get away from it, for every struggle against lust using only one's own strength is doomed to failure.

Dietrich Bonhoeffer

Every time we are tempted in life, it will be by something immediate. It will be something that will suggest to us that we need to postpone the more important for the more urgent.

Franklin Graham

Sin is an allergic reaction to God's law, an irrational anti-God syndrome that drives us to exalt ourselves and steels our heart against devotion and obedience to our Maker.

J. I. Packer

The higher the hill, the stronger the wind: so the loftier the life, the stronger the enemy's temptations.

John Wycliffe

GOD'S WORDS OF WISDOM

*No temptation has seized you except what is common to man.
And God is faithful; he will not let you be tempted beyond
what you can bear. But when you are tempted, he will also
provide a way out so that you can stand up under it.*

1 Corinthians 10:13 NIV

The Lord knows how to deliver the godly out of temptations.

2 Peter 2:9 NKJV

*Put on the whole armor of God, that you may be able to stand
against the wiles of the devil.*

Ephesians 6:11 NKJV

*This High Priest of ours understands our weaknesses, for he
faced all of the same temptations we do, yet he did not sin.*

Hebrews 4:15 NLT

SUMMING IT UP

Because you live in a temptation-filled world, you must
guard your eyes, your thoughts, and your heart—all day,
every day.

GUARD YOUR EYES AGAINST MATERIALISM

Do not love the world or the things in the world.
If anyone loves the world, the love of the Father is not in him.

1 John 2:15 NKJV

How important are your material possessions? Not as important as you might think. In the life of a committed Christian, material possessions should play a rather small role. In fact, when we become overly enamored with the things we own, we needlessly distance ourselves from the peace that God offers to those who place Him at the center of their lives.

Of course, we all need the basic necessities of life, but once we meet those needs for ourselves and for our families, the piling up of possessions creates more problems than it solves. Our real riches, of course, are not of this world. We are never really rich until we are rich in spirit.

Do you find yourself wrapped up in the concerns of the material world? If so, it's time to reorder your priorities by turning your thoughts and your prayers to more important matters. And, it's time to begin storing up riches that will endure throughout eternity: the spiritual kind.

And He told them, "Watch out and be on guard against all greed, because one's life is not in the abundance of his possessions."

Luke 12:15 Holman CSB

A TIP FOR GUARDING YOUR HEART

Do you find yourself wrapped up in the material world? If so, it's time to reorder your priorities and reassess your values. Today, think long and hard about the priorities and values that guide your decision-making.

WORDS OF WISDOM

If you want to be truly happy, you won't find it on an endless quest for more stuff. You'll find it in receiving God's generosity and then passing that generosity along.

Bill Hybels

The Scriptures also reveal a warning that if we are consumed with greed, not only do we disobey God, but we will miss the opportunity to allow Him to use us as instruments for others.

Charles Stanley

There is absolutely no evidence that complexity and materialism lead to happiness. On the contrary, there is plenty of evidence that simplicity and spirituality lead to joy, a blessedness that is better than happiness.

Dennis Swanberg

The cross is laid on every Christian. It begins with the call to abandon the attachments of this world.

Dietrich Bonhoeffer

A society that pursues pleasure runs the risk of raising expectations ever higher, so that true contentment always lies tantalizingly out of reach.

Philip Yancey and Paul Brand

GOD'S WORDS OF WISDOM

He who trusts in his riches will fall, but the righteous will flourish . . . .

Proverbs 11:28 NKJV

No one can serve two masters. The person will hate one master and love the other, or will follow one master and refuse to follow the other. You cannot serve both God and worldly riches.

Matthew 6:24 NCV

Since we entered the world penniless and will leave it penniless, if we have bread on the table and shoes on our feet, that's enough.

1 Timothy 6:7-8 MSG

SUMMING IT UP

Material possessions may seem appealing at first, but they pale in comparison to the spiritual gifts that God gives to those who put Him first. Count yourself among that number.

GUARD YOUR EYES AGAINST THE MEDIA

Don't copy the behavior and customs of this world,
but let God transform you into a new person by changing
the way you think. Then you will know what
God wants you to do, and you will know how good
and pleasing and perfect his will really is.

Romans 12:2 NLT

I f you and your loved ones have acquired the bad habit of watching whatever happens to pop up on your family's TV screen, it's time to rethink the way you control your clicker. Most television networks (as well as the other forms of popular media) can be dangerous to your emotional and spiritual health.

The media is working around the clock in an attempt to rearrange your family's priorities in ways that are definitely not in your best interests. The media is trying to teach your family that physical appearance is all-important, that material possessions should be acquired at any cost, and that the world operates independently of God's laws. But guess what? Those messages are lies.

In the pursuit of profits, the media glamorizes violence, exploits suffering, and sensationalizes sex, all in the name of "ratings" (translated: "money").

So here's a question for you and your family: Will you control what appears on your TV screen, or will you be controlled by it? If you're willing to take complete control over the images that appear inside the four walls of your home, you'll be doing yourselves a king-sized favor. So forget the media hype, and pay attention to God. Stand up for Him and be counted, not just in church where it's relatively easy to be a Christian, but also when you're deciding what to watch. You owe it to your Creator . . . and you owe it to yourselves.

A TIP FOR GUARDING YOUR HEART

Don't trust the media's messages. Many of the messages that you receive from the media are specifically designed to sell you products that interfere with your spiritual, physical, or emotional health. God takes great interest in your health; the moguls from Madison Avenue take great interest in your pocketbook. Trust God.

WORDS OF WISDOM

The true Christian, though he is in revolt against the world's efforts to brainwash him, is no mere rebel for rebellion's sake. He dissents from the world because he knows that it cannot make good on its promises.

A. W. Tozer

Every day, I find countless opportunities to decide whether I will obey God and demonstrate my love for Him or try to please myself or the world system. God is waiting for my choices.

Bill Bright

Too many Christians have geared their program to please, to entertain, and to gain favor from this world. We are concerned with how much, instead of how little, like this age we can become.

Billy Graham

Tell me that you love the world, and I will tell you that love of the world is enmity to God.

C. H. Spurgeon

Aim at heaven and you will get earth thrown in; aim at earth and you will get neither.

C. S. Lewis

GOD'S WORDS OF WISDOM

Let no one deceive himself. If anyone among you seems to be wise in this age, let him become a fool that he may become wise. For the wisdom of this world is foolishness with God. For it is written, "He catches the wise in their own craftiness."

1 Corinthians 3:18–19 NKJV

Do not love the world or the things in the world. If you love the world, the love of the Father is not in you.

1 John 2:15 NCV

For whatever is born of God overcomes the world. And this is the victory that has overcome the world—our faith.

1 John 5:4 NKJV

Religion that God our Father accepts as pure and faultless is this: to look after orphans and widows in their distress and to keep oneself from being polluted by the world.

James 1:27 NIV

SUMMING IT UP

The popular media has a way of attacking your senses and your heart. Approach the media with care.

GUARD YOUR EYES AGAINST ENVY

But if you harbor bitter envy and selfish ambition in your hearts, do not boast about it or deny the truth. Such "wisdom" does not come down from heaven but is earthly, unspiritual, of the devil. For where you have envy and selfish ambition, there you find disorder and every evil practice.

James 3:14-17 NIV

In a competitive, cut-throat world, it is easy to become envious of other's success. But it's wrong.

We know intuitively that envy is wrong, but because we are frail, imperfect human beings, we may find ourselves struggling with feelings of envy or resentment, or both. These feelings may be especially forceful when we see other people experience unusually good fortune.

Have you recently felt the pangs of envy creeping into your heart? If so, it's time to focus on the marvelous things that God has done for you and your family. And just as importantly, you must refrain from preoccupying yourself with the blessings that God has chosen to give others.

So here's a surefire formula for a happier, healthier life: Count your own blessings and let your neighbors count theirs. It's the godly way to live.

We must not become conceited,
provoking one another,
envying one another.

Galatians 5:26 Holman CSB

A Tip for Guarding Your Heart

Feelings of envy will rob you of happiness and peace. Don't allow yourself to be robbed.

WORDS OF WISDOM

How can you possess the miseries of envy when you possess in Christ the best of all portions?

C. H. Spurgeon

When you worry about what you don't have, you won't be able to enjoy what you do have.

Charles Swindoll

Contentment comes when we develop an attitude of gratitude for the important things we do have in our lives that we tend to take for granted if we have our eyes staring longingly at our neighbor's stuff.

Dave Ramsey

Too many Christians envy the sinners their pleasure and the saints their joy because they don't have either one.

Martin Luther

As a moth gnaws a garment, so does envy consume a man.

St. John Chrysostom

GOD'S WORDS OF WISDOM

Do not covet your neighbor's house . . . or anything that belongs to your neighbor.

Exodus 20:17 Holman CSB

Stop your anger! Turn from your rage! Do not envy others—it only leads to harm.

Psalm 37:8 NLT

If your sinful nature controls your mind, there is death. But if the Holy Spirit controls your mind, there is life and peace.

Romans 8:6 NLT

I have told you these things, so that in me you may have peace. In this world you will have trouble. But take heart! I have overcome the world.

John 16:33 NIV

SUMMING IT UP

Envy is a sin, a sin that robs you of contentment and peace. So you must refuse to let feelings of envy invade your thoughts or your heart.

GUARD YOUR EYES AGAINST IMMORALITY

You have heard that the law of Moses says,
"Do not commit adultery." But I say, anyone who even looks
at a woman with lust in his eye
has already committed adultery with her in his heart.

Matthew 5:27-28 NLT

You know that you should guard your heart against immorality, but sometimes it's hard to do. Have you noticed that the world is filled to the brim with temptations? Unless you've been living the life of a hermit, you've observed that temptations, both great and small, are everywhere.

Some temptations are small; eating a second scoop of ice cream, for example, is tempting, but not very dangerous. Other temptations, however, are not nearly so harmless. And when you are faced with temptations that threaten to compromise the moral standards that have been spelled out in God's Holy Word, you must run (not walk) in the opposite direction.

The devil is working 24 hours a day, and he's causing pain and heartache in more ways than ever before. Thankfully, in the battle against Satan, you are never alone. God is always with you, and He gives you the power to resist temptation whenever you ask Him for the strength to do so.

In a letter to believers, Peter offered a stern warning: "Your adversary the devil walks about like a roaring lion, seeking whom he may devour" (1 Peter 5:8 NKJV). As a believer, you must heed that warning, and you must behave accordingly.

All who indulge in a sinful life are
dangerously lawless,
for sin is a major disruption of God's order.

1 John 3:4 MSG

A TIP FOR GUARDING YOUR HEART

Sometimes immorality is obvious and sometimes it's not. So beware: the most subtle forms of sin are often the most dangerous.

WORDS OF WISDOM

How little people know who think that holiness is dull.
When one meets the real thing, it's irresistible.

C. S. Lewis

God is not morally neutral.

Francis Schaeffer

We pursue righteousness when we flee the things that
keep us from following the Lord Jesus. These are the keys:
flee, follow, and fight.

Franklin Graham

Let God use times of waiting to mold and shape your
character. Let God use those times to purify your life and
make you into a clean vessel for His service.

Henry Blackaby and Claude King

You don't have to be like the world to have an impact on
the world. You don't have to be like the crowd to change
the crowd. You don't have to lower yourself down to their
level to lift them up to your level. Holiness doesn't seek to
be odd. Holiness seeks to be like God.

Max Lucado

GOD'S WORDS OF WISDOM

*If we say that we have no sin, we deceive ourselves, and
the truth is not in us. If we confess our sins, He is faithful
and just to forgive us our sins and to cleanse us from all
unrighteousness.*

1 John 1:8-9 NKJV

*Whoever transgresses and does not abide in the doctrine of
Christ does not have God. He who abides in the doctrine of
Christ has both the Father and the Son.*

2 John 1:9 NKJV

*Let us lay aside every weight, and the sin which so easily
ensnares us, and let us run with endurance the race that is set
before us.*

Hebrews 12:1 NKJV

SUMMING IT UP

Sin has the power to destroy the things you hold dear,
starting, of course, with your family. So you must never
let down your guard.

PART 3

GUARD
YOUR STEPS

*Mark out a straight path for your feet;
then stick to the path and stay safe.
Don't get sidetracked;
keep your feet from following evil.*

Proverbs 4:26-27 NLT

Guard Your Steps by Making a Straight Path

Mark out a straight path for your feet;
then stick to the path and stay safe.

Proverbs 4:26 NLT

I f you desire to guard your heart, you must choose a path that is pleasing to God, but you'll be tempted to choose a different path. If you're like most people, you seek the admiration of your neighbors, your coworkers, and your family members. But the eagerness to please others should never overshadow your eagerness to please God. If you seek to fulfill the purposes that God has in store for you, then you must be a "doer of the word." And how can you do so? By putting God first.

The words of Matthew 6:33 make it clear: "But seek first the kingdom of God and His righteousness, and all these things will be provided for you" (Holman CSB). God has given you a priceless guidebook, an indispensable tool for "seeking His kingdom." That tool, of course, is the

Holy Bible. It contains thorough instructions which, if followed, lead to fulfillment, righteousness, and salvation.

But for those who would ignore God's Word, Martin Luther issued this warning: "You may as well quit reading and hearing the Word of God and give it to the devil if you do not desire to live according to it." He understood that obedience leads to abundance just as surely as disobedience leads to disaster; you should understand it, too.

Each new day presents countless opportunities to put God in first place . . . or not. When you honor Him by living according to His commandments, you earn the abundance and peace that He promises. But, if you ignore God's teachings, you will inevitably bring needless suffering upon yourself and your family.

Would you like a time-tested formula for successful living? Here it is: Don't just listen to God's Word, live by it. Does this sound too simple? Perhaps it is simple, but it is also the only way to reap the marvelous riches that God has in store for you.

A TIP FOR GUARDING YOUR HEART

Ask yourself if your behavior has been radically changed by your unfolding relationship with God. It the answer to this question is unclear to you—or if the honest answer is a resounding no—think of a single step you can take, a positive change in your life, that will bring you closer to your Creator.

WORDS OF WISDOM

The temptation of the age is to look good without being good.

Brennan Manning

After you receive Christ, you will continue to repent as you grow in Christian faith and character. This repentance is a change of mind that leads to change of behavior.

Charles Stanley

More depends on my walk than my talk.

D. L. Moody

I have found that the closer I am to the godly people around me, the easier it is for me to live a righteous life because they hold me accountable.

John MacArthur

He who prays as he ought, will endeavor to live as he prays.

John Owen

GOD'S WORDS OF WISDOM

In everything set them an example by doing what is good.

Titus 2:7 NIV

Are there those among you who are truly wise and understanding? Then they should show it by living right and doing good things with a gentleness that comes from wisdom.

James 3:13 NCV

Even a child is known by his actions, by whether his conduct is pure and right.

Proverbs 20:11 NIV

Here is a simple, rule-of-thumb for behavior: Ask yourself what you want people to do for you, then grab the initiative and do it for them. Add up God's Law and Prophets and this is what you get.

Matthew 7:12 MSG

SUMMING IT UP

How can you guard your steps? By walking with Jesus every day of your life.

GUARD YOUR STEPS BY LEADING A DISCIPLINED LIFESTYLE

Discipline yourself for the purpose of godliness.

1 Timothy 4:7 NASB

God doesn't reward laziness, misbehavior, or apathy. To the contrary, He expects believers to behave with dignity and discipline. God's Word reminds us again and again that our Creator expects us to lead disciplined lives—and we must take God at His Word, despite temptations to do otherwise.

We live in a world in which leisure is glorified and indifference is often glamorized. But God has other plans. He did not create us for lives of mediocrity; He created us for far greater things.

Life's greatest rewards seldom fall into our laps; to the contrary, our greatest accomplishments usually require lots of work, which is perfectly fine with God. After all, He knows that we're up to the task, and He has big plans for us; may we, as disciplined believers, always be worthy of those plans.

He who heeds discipline shows the way to life,
but whoever ignores correction
leads others astray.

Proverbs 10:17 NIV

A TIP FOR GUARDING YOUR HEART

Be disciplined in your own approach to life. You can't teach it if you won't live it.

WORDS OF WISDOM

The Bible calls for discipline and a recognition of authority. Children must learn this at home.

Billy Graham

Discipline is training that develops and corrects.

Charles Stanley

Work is doing it. Discipline is doing it every day. Diligence is doing it well every day.

Dave Ramsey

God cannot build character without our cooperation. If we resist Him, then He chastens us into submission. But, if we submit to Him, then He can accomplish His work. He is not satisfied with a halfway job. God wants a perfect work; He wants a finished product that is mature and complete.

Warren Wiersbe

As we seek to become disciples of Jesus Christ, we should never forget that the word *disciple* is directly related to the word *discipline*. To be a disciple of the Lord Jesus Christ is to know his discipline.

Dennis Swanberg

GOD'S WORDS OF WISDOM

Do you not know that those who run in a race all run, but only one receives the prize? Run in such a way that you may win. Everyone who competes in the games exercises self-control in all things.

1 Corinthians 9:24-25 NASB

I discipline my body and make it my slave.

1 Corinthians 9:27 NASB

God hasn't invited us into a disorderly, unkempt life but into something holy and beautiful—as beautiful on the inside as the outside.

1 Thessalonians 4:7 MSG

Folly is loud; she is undisciplined and without knowledge.

Proverbs 9:13 NIV

SUMMING IT UP

If you choose to lead a disciplined lifestyle, your steps will be protected. If you choose to lead an undisciplined lifestyle, your steps will be misdirected.

GUARD YOUR STEPS BY TRUSTING GOD'S PLAN

The Lord says, "I will guide you along the best pathway for your life. I will advise you and watch over you."

Psalm 32:8 NLT

God has plans for your life. Big plans. But He won't force you to follow His will; to the contrary, He has given you free will, the ability to make decisions on your own. With the freedom to choose comes the responsibility of living with the consequences of the choices you make.

The most important decision of your life is, of course, your commitment to accept Jesus Christ as your personal Lord and Savior. And once your eternal destiny is secured, you will undoubtedly ask yourself the question "What now, Lord?" If you earnestly seek God's will for your life, you will find it . . . in time.

When you make the decision to seek God's will for your life, you will contemplate His Word, and you will be watchful for His signs. You will associate with fellow believers who will encourage your spiritual growth. And, you will listen to that inner voice that speaks to you in the quiet moments of your daily devotionals.

Sometimes, God's plans are crystal clear, but other times, He leads you through the wilderness before He delivers you to the Promised Land. So be patient, keep searching, and keep praying. If you do, then in time, God will answer your prayers and make His plans known.

God is right here, and He intends to use you in wonderful, unexpected ways. You'll discover those plans by doing things His way . . . and you'll be eternally grateful that you did.

A TIP FOR GUARDING YOUR HEART

Big, bigger, and very big plans. God has very big plans in store for your life, so trust Him and wait patiently for those plans to unfold. And remember: God's timing is best.

WORDS OF WISDOM

All God's plans have the mark of the cross on them, and all His plans have death to self in them.

E. M. Bounds

God surrounds you with opportunity. You and I are free in Jesus Christ, not to do whatever we want, but to be all that God wants us to be.

Warren Wiersbe

The Almighty does nothing without reason, although the frail mind of man cannot explain the reason.

St. Augustine

Do not let Satan deceive you into being afraid of God's plans for your life.

R. A. Torrey

God will not permit any troubles to come upon us unless He has a specific plan by which great blessing can come out of the difficulty.

Peter Marshall

GOD'S WORDS OF WISDOM

"I say this because I know what I am planning for you," says the Lord. "I have good plans for you, not plans to hurt you. I will give you hope and a good future."

Jeremiah 29:11 NCV

People may make plans in their minds, but the Lord decides what they will do.

Proverbs 16:9 NCV

There is no wisdom, no insight, no plan that can succeed against the Lord.

Proverbs 21:30 NIV

He replied, "Every plant that My heavenly Father didn't plant will be uprooted."

Matthew 15:13 Holman CSB

SUMMING IT UP

God has a plan for your life. Your job is to discover that plan and follow it.

GUARD YOUR HEART WITH DAILY DEVOTIONALS

Morning by morning he wakens me
and opens my understanding to his will.
The Sovereign Lord has spoken to me, and I have listened.

Isaiah 50:4-5 NLT

Each new day is a gift from God, and if we are wise, we will spend a few quiet moments each morning thanking the Giver. When we begin each day with heads bowed and hearts lifted, we remind ourselves of God's love, His protection, and His commandments. And if we are wise, we align our priorities for the coming day with the teachings and commandments that God has given us through His Holy Word.

The path to spiritual maturity unfolds day by day. Each day offers the opportunity to worship God, to ignore God, or to rebel against God. When we worship Him with our prayers, our words, our thoughts, and our actions, we are blessed by the richness of our relationship with the Father. But if we ignore God altogether or intentionally rebel against His commandments, we rob ourselves of His blessings.

Today offers yet another opportunity for spiritual growth. If you choose, you can seize that opportunity by obeying God's Word, by seeking His will, and by walking with His Son.

Are you seeking to change some aspect of your life? Do you seek to improve the condition of your spiritual, physical, emotional, or financial health? If so, ask for God's help and ask for it many times each day . . . starting with your morning devotional.

A TIP FOR GUARDING YOUR HEART

If you're wise, you'll place a high priority on spending quiet time with God each day. If you can't find time for God, then it's time to give your "to-do" list a major overhaul.

WORDS OF WISDOM

Devotional books have an important ministry, but they are never substitutes for your Bible.

Warren Wiersbe

Half an hour of listening to God is essential except when one is very busy. Then, a full hour is needed.

St. Francis of Sales

We must appropriate the tender mercy of God every day after conversion or problems quickly develop. We need his grace daily in order to live a righteous life.

Jim Cymbala

Whatever is your best time in the day, give that to communion with God.

Hudson Taylor

If we really believe not only that God exists but also that God is actively present in our lives—healing, teaching, and guiding—we need to set aside a time and space to give God our undivided attention.

Henri Nouwen

GOD'S WORDS OF WISDOM

It is good to give thanks to the Lord, to sing praises to the Most High. It is good to proclaim your unfailing love in the morning, your faithfulness in the evening.

Psalm 92:1-2 NLT

May the words of my mouth and the thoughts of my heart be pleasing to you, O Lord, my rock and my redeemer.

Psalm 19:14 NLT

Truly my soul silently waits for God; from Him comes my salvation.

Psalm 62:1 NKJV

But grow in the grace and knowledge of our Lord and Savior Jesus Christ. To Him be the glory both now and to the day of eternity.

2 Peter 3:18 Holman CSB

SUMMING IT UP

You need a regular appointment with your Creator. God is ready to talk to you, and you should prepare yourself each morning to talk to Him.

GUARD YOUR STEPS BY SETTING A GOOD EXAMPLE

*Be an example to the believers in word, in conduct,
in love, in spirit, in faith, in purity.*

1 Timothy 4:12 NKJV

As followers of Christ, each of us must ask ourselves an important question: "What kind of example am I?" The answer to that question determines, in large part, whether or not we are positive influences on our own little corners of the world.

Are you the kind of friend whose life serves as a powerful example of righteousness? Are you a person whose behavior serves as a positive role model for young people? Are you the kind of Christian whose actions, day in and day out, are based upon integrity, fidelity, and a love for the Lord? If so, you are not only blessed by God, but you are also a powerful force for good in a world that desperately needs positive influences such as yours.

Phillips Brooks advised, "Be such a person, and live such a life, that if every person were such as you, and every life a life like yours, this earth would be God's Paradise." And that's sound advice because our families and friends are watching . . . and, for that matter, so is God.

In every way be an example
of doing good deeds.
When you teach,
do it with honesty and seriousness.

Titus 2:7 NCV

A TIP FOR GUARDING YOUR HEART

Your life is a sermon. What kind of sermon will you preach? The words you choose to speak may have some impact on others, but not nearly as much impact as the life you choose to live.

WORDS OF WISDOM

Integrity of heart is indispensable.

John Calvin

If I take care of my character, my reputation will take care of itself.

D. L. Moody

There is no way to grow a saint overnight. Character, like the oak tree, does not spring up like a mushroom.

Vance Havner

You can never separate a leader's actions from his character.

John Maxwell

The sermon of your life in tough times ministers to people more powerfully than the most eloquent speaker.

Bill Bright

GOD'S WORDS OF WISDOM

We have around us many people whose lives tell us what faith means. So let us run the race that is before us and never give up. We should remove from our lives anything that would get in the way and the sin that so easily holds us back.

Hebrews 12:1 NCV

You are the light that gives light to the world. . . . In the same way, you should be a light for other people. Live so that they will see the good things you do and will praise your Father in heaven.

Matthew 5:14,16 NCV

Do you want to be counted wise, to build a reputation for wisdom? Here's what you do: Live well, live wisely, live humbly. It's the way you live, not the way you talk, that counts.

James 3:13 MSG

SUMMING IT UP

God wants you to be a good example to your family, to your friends, and to the world.

GUARD YOUR STEPS WITH WISE PRIORITIES

*It's obvious, isn't it? The place where your treasure is,
is the place you will most want to be, and end up being.*

Luke 12:34 MSG

On your daily to-do list, all items are not created equal: Certain tasks are extremely important while others are not. Therefore, it's imperative that you prioritize your daily activities and complete each task in the approximate order of its importance.

The principle of doing first things first is simple in theory but more complicated in practice. Well-meaning family, friends, and coworkers have a way of making unexpected demands upon your time. Furthermore, each day has its own share of minor emergencies; these urgent matters tend to draw your attention away from more important ones. On paper, prioritizing is simple, but to act upon those priorities in the real world requires maturity, patience, determination, and balance.

If you fail to prioritize your day, life will automatically do the job for you. So your choice is simple: prioritize or be prioritized. It's a choice that will help determine the quality of your life.

If you're having trouble balancing the many demands of everyday living, perhaps you've been trying to organize your life according to your own plans, not God's. A better strategy, of course, is to take your daily obligations and place them in the hands of the One who created you. To do so, you must prioritize your day according to God's commandments, and you must seek His will and His wisdom in all matters. Then, you can face the coming day with the assurance that the same God who created our universe out of nothingness will help you place first things first in your own life.

Are you living a balanced life that allows time for worship, for family, for work, for exercise, and a little time left over for you? Or do you feel overworked, under-appreciated, overwhelmed, and underpaid? If your to-do list is "maxed out" and your energy is on the wane, it's time to restore a sense of balance to your life. You can do so by turning the concerns and the priorities of this day over to God—prayerfully, earnestly, and often. Then, you must listen for His answer . . . and trust the answer He gives.

WORDS OF WISDOM

Don't stop the plough to kill a mouse. Do not hinder important business for the discussion of a trifle.

C. H. Spurgeon

Wife and family come before business, ministry, or career. God comes before wife and family.

Edwin Louis Cole

The essence of the Christian life is Jesus: that in all things He might have the preeminence, not that in some things He might have a place.

Franklin Graham

Often our lives are strangled by things that don't ultimately matter.

Grady Nutt

A TIP FOR GUARDING YOUR HEART

Setting priorities may mean saying no. You don't have time to do everything, so it's perfectly okay to say no to the things that mean less so that you'll have time for the things that mean more.

GOD'S WORDS OF WISDOM

And I pray this: that your love will keep on growing in knowledge and every kind of discernment, so that you can determine what really matters and can be pure and blameless in the day of Christ.

Philippians 1:9 Holman CSB

He said to them all, "If anyone desires to come after Me, let him deny himself, and take up his cross daily, and follow Me. For whoever desires to save his life will lose it, but whoever loses his life for My sake will save it."

Luke 9:23-24 NKJV

Let us fix our eyes on Jesus, the author and perfecter of our faith, who for the joy set before him endured the cross, scorning its shame, and sat down at the right hand of the throne of God.

Hebrews 12:2 NIV

SUMMING IT UP

Your Heavenly Father wants you to prioritize your day and your life. And the best place to start is by putting God first.

GUARD YOUR STEPS WITH WISDOM

How much better to get wisdom than gold!
And to get understanding is to be chosen rather than silver.

Proverbs 16:16 NKJV

Do you place a high value on the acquisition of wisdom? If so, you are not alone; most people would like to be wise, but not everyone is willing to do the work that is required to become wise. Wisdom is not like a mushroom; it does not spring up overnight. It is, instead, like an oak tree that starts as a tiny acorn, grows into a sapling, and eventually reaches up to the sky, tall and strong.

To become wise, you must seek God's guidance and live according to His Word. To become wise, you must seek instruction with consistency and purpose. To become wise, you must not only learn the lessons of the Christian life, but you must also live by them. But oftentimes, that's easier said than done.

Sometimes, amid the demands of daily life, you will lose perspective. Life may seem out of balance, and the pressures of everyday living may seem overwhelming. What's needed is a fresh perspective, a restored sense of balance . . . and God's wisdom. If you call upon the Lord and seek to see the world through His eyes, He will give you guidance, wisdom, and perspective. When you make God's priorities your priorities, He will lead you according to His plan and according to His commandments. When you study God's teachings, you are reminded that God's reality is the ultimate reality.

Do you seek to live a life of righteousness and wisdom? If so, you must study the ultimate source of wisdom: the Word of God. You must seek out worthy mentors and listen carefully to their advice. You must associate, day in and day out, with godly men and women. Then, as you accumulate wisdom, you must not keep it for yourself; you must, instead, share it with your friends and family members.

But be forewarned: if you sincerely seek to share your hard-earned wisdom with others, your actions must reflect the values that you hold dear. The best way to share your wisdom—perhaps the only way—is not by your words, but by your example.

A TIP FOR GUARDING YOUR HEART

Need wisdom? God's got it. If you want it, then study God's Word and associate with godly people.

WORDS OF WISDOM

Don't expect wisdom to come into your life like great chunks of rock on a conveyor belt. Wisdom comes privately from God as a byproduct of right decisions, godly reactions, and the application of spiritual principles to daily circumstances.

Charles Swindoll

Knowledge is horizontal. Wisdom is vertical; it comes down from above.

Billy Graham

God's plan for our guidance is for us to grow gradually in wisdom before we get to the cross roads.

Bill Hybels

The more wisdom enters our hearts, the more we will be able to trust our hearts in difficult situations.

John Eldredge

Patience is the companion of wisdom.

St. Augustine

GOD'S WORDS OF WISDOM

The Lord says, "I will make you wise and show you where to go. I will guide you and watch over you."

Psalm 32:8 NCV

Wisdom is the principal thing; therefore get wisdom. And in all your getting, get understanding.

Proverbs 4:7 NKJV

Happy is the person who finds wisdom, the one who gets understanding.

Proverbs 3:13 NCV

Anyone who listens to my teaching and obeys me is wise, like a person who builds a house on solid rock. Though the rain comes in torrents and the floodwaters rise and the winds beat against that house, it won't collapse, because it is built on rock.

Matthew 7:24–25 NLT

SUMMING IT UP

If you own a Bible, you have ready access to God's wisdom. Your job is to read, to understand, and to apply His teachings to your life . . . starting now and ending never.

GUARD YOUR STEPS WITH YOUR FAMILY

Choose for yourselves today the one you will worship . . . .
As for me and my family, we will worship the Lord.

Joshua 24:15 Holman CSB

I n a world filled with countless obligations and frequent frustrations, we may be tempted to take our families for granted. But God intends otherwise.

Our families are precious gifts from our Father in heaven. If we are to be the righteous men that God intends, we must care for our families, we must love our families, we must lead our families, and we must make time for our families, even when the demands of the day are great.

No family is perfect, and neither is yours. But, despite the inevitable challenges, obligations, and hurt feelings of family life, your clan is God's blessing to you. That little band of men, women, kids, and babies is a priceless treasure on temporary loan from the Father above. Give thanks to the Giver for the gift of family . . . and act accordingly.

Love must be without hypocrisy.
Detest evil; cling to what is good.
Show family affection to one another
with brotherly love.
Outdo one another in showing honor.

Romans 12:9–10 Holman CSB

A TIP FOR GUARDING YOUR HEART

If you're lucky enough to be a member of a loving, supportive family, then you owe it to yourself—and to them—to share your thoughts, your hopes, your encouragement, and your love.

WORDS OF WISDOM

At the end, only two things really matter to a man, regardless of who he is, and they are the affection and understanding of his family.

Admiral Richard Byrd

As the first community to which a person is attached and the first authority under which a person learns to live, the family establishes society's most basic values.

Charles Colson

A family is a place where principles are hammered and honed on the anvil of everyday living.

Charles Swindoll

Sadly, family problems and even financial problems are seldom the real problem, but often the symptom of a weak or nonexistent value system.

Dave Ramsey

Calm and peaceful, the home should be the one place where people are certain they will be welcomed, received, protected, and loved.

Ed Young

GOD'S WORDS OF WISDOM

Their first responsibility is to show godliness at home and repay their parents by taking care of them. This is something that pleases God very much.

1 Timothy 5:4 NLT

Every kingdom divided against itself will be ruined, and every city or household divided against itself will not stand.

Matthew 12:25 NIV

Let love and faithfulness never leave you . . . write them on the tablet of your heart.

Proverbs 3:3 NIV

He who brings trouble on his family will inherit only wind . . . .

Proverbs 11:29 NIV

SUMMING IT UP

Your family is a precious gift from above, a gift that should be treasured, nurtured, and loved.

GUARD YOUR STEPS WITH GODLY FRIENDS

As iron sharpens iron, a friend sharpens a friend.

Proverbs 27:17 NLT

Make no mistake: your friends can help you guard your steps—and it's up to you to let them. The dictionary defines the word "friend" as "a person who is attached to another by feelings of affection or personal regard." This definition is accurate, as far as it goes, but when we examine the deeper meaning of friendship, many more descriptors come to mind: trustworthiness, loyalty, helpfulness, kindness, understanding, forgiveness, encouragement, humor, and cheerfulness, to mention but a few. Needless to say, our trusted friends and family members can help us discover God's unfolding purposes for our lives. Our task is to enlist our friends' wisdom, their cooperation, their honesty, and their encouragement.

As you consider the many blessings that God has given you, remember to thank Him for the friends He has chosen to place along your path. Seek their guidance, and, when asked, never withhold yours. Then, as you travel through life with trusted companions by your side, you will bless them, and they will richly bless you.

Loyal Christian friendship is ordained by God. Throughout the Bible, we are reminded to love one another, to care for one another, and to treat one another as we wish to be treated. So remember the important role that Christian friendship plays in God's plans for His kingdom and for your life. Resolve to be a trustworthy, loyal friend. And, treasure the people in your life who are loyal friends to you. Friendship is, after all, a glorious gift, praised by God. Give thanks for that gift and nurture it.

Beloved, if God so loved us,
we also ought to love one another.

1 John 4:11 NKJV

A TIP FOR GUARDING YOUR HEART

Today, as you think about the nature and the quality of your friendships, remember the first rule of making (and keeping) friends: it's the Golden Rule, and it starts like this: "Do unto others . . . ."

WORDS OF WISDOM

I have found that the closer I am to the godly people around me, the easier it is for me to live a righteous life because they hold me accountable.

John MacArthur

Yes, the Spirit was sent to be our Counselor. Yes, Jesus speaks to us personally. But often he works through another human being.

John Eldredge

God has not called us to see through each other, but to see each other through.

Jess Moody

When we honestly ask ourselves which person in our lives means the most to us, we often find that it is he who, instead of giving much advice, solutions, and cures, has chosen rather to share our pain and touch our wounds with a gentle and tender hand. The friend who can be silent with us in a moment of despair or confusion, who can stay with us in an hour of grief and bereavement, who can tolerate not knowing, not curing, not healing, and face us with the reality of our powerlessness, that is a friend who cares.

Henri Nouwen

GOD'S WORDS OF WISDOM

Greater love has no one than this, that he lay down his life for his friends.

John 15:13 NIV

A friend loves you all the time, and a brother helps in time of trouble.

Proverbs 17:17 NCV

If a fellow believer hurts you, go and tell him—work it out between the two of you. If he listens, you've made a friend.

Matthew 18:15 MSG

Finally, all of you be of one mind, having compassion for one another; love as brothers, be tenderhearted, be courteous.

1 Peter 3:8 NKJV

SUMMING IT UP

Thank your Creator God for the godly friends He has placed along your path. Cherish those friendships, and do your best to make them flourish.

GUARD YOUR STEPS BY PLANNING WISELY

The plans of the diligent certainly lead to profit,
but anyone who is reckless only becomes poor.

Proverbs 21:5 Holman CSB

A re you willing to plan for the future—and are you willing to work diligently to accomplish the plans that you've made? If you desire to reap a bountiful harvest from life, you should plan for the future (by crafting a "to-do list for life") while entrusting the final outcome to God. Then, you should do your part to make the future better (by working dutifully), while acknowledging the sovereignty of God's hands over all affairs, including your own.

As you make plans and establish priorities, remember this: you're not the only one working on your behalf: God, too, is at work. And with Him as your partner, your ultimate success is guaranteed.

God has big plans for your life, wonderful, surprising plans . . . but He won't force those plans upon you. To the contrary, He has given you free will, the ability to make decisions on your own. Now, it's up to you to make those decisions wisely.

If you seek to live in accordance with God's plan for your life, you will study His Word, you will be attentive to His instructions, and you will be watchful for His signs. You will associate with fellow believers who, by their words and actions, will encourage your spiritual growth. You will assiduously avoid those two terrible temptations: the temptation to sin and the temptation to squander time. And finally, you will listen carefully, even reverently, to the conscience that God has placed in your heart.

God intends to use you in wonderful, unexpected ways if you let Him. Your job, of course, is to let Him.

*Commit to the Lord whatever you do,
and your plans will succeed.*

Proverbs 16:3 NIV

A TIP FOR GUARDING YOUR HEART

Think ahead—it's the best way of making sure you don't get left behind.

WORDS OF WISDOM

Plan your work. Without a system, you'll feel swamped.

Norman Vincent Peale

God has a plan for your life . . . do you?

Jim Gallery

The only way you can experience abundant life is to surrender your plans to Him.

Charles Stanley

Allow your dreams a place in your prayers and plans. God-given dreams can help you move into the future He is preparing for you.

Barbara Johnson

Plan ahead—it wasn't raining when Noah built the ark.

Anonymous

GOD'S WORDS OF WISDOM

May he give you the desire of your heart and make all your plans succeed.

Psalm 20:4 NIV

Plans fail for lack of counsel, but with many advisors, they succeed.

Proverbs 15:22 NIV

A prudent person foresees the danger ahead and takes precautions. The simpleton goes blindly on and suffers the consequences.

Proverbs 27:12 NLT

But the noble man makes noble plans, and by noble deeds he stands.

Isaiah 32:8 NIV

SUMMING IT UP

It isn't that complicated: If you plan your steps carefully, and if you follow your plan conscientiously, you will probably succeed. If you don't, you probably won't.

GUARD YOUR STEPS BY LIVING PURPOSEFULLY

You will show me the path of life;
in Your presence is fullness of joy;
at Your right hand are pleasures forevermore.

Psalm 16:11 NKJV

God has things He wants you to do and places He wants you to go. The most important decision of your life is, of course, your commitment to accept Jesus Christ as your personal Lord and Savior. And, once your eternal destiny is secured, you will undoubtedly ask yourself the question "What now, Lord?" If you earnestly seek God's will for your life, you will find it . . . in time.

As you prayerfully consider God's path for your life, you should study His Word and be ever watchful for His signs. You should associate with fellow believers who will encourage your spiritual growth, and you should listen to that inner voice that speaks to you in the quiet moments of your daily devotionals.

As you continually seek God's purpose for your life, be patient: your Heavenly Father may not always reveal Himself as quickly as you would like. But rest assured: God is here, and He intends to use you in wonderful, unexpected ways. He desires to lead you along a path of His choosing. Your challenge is to watch, to listen . . . and to follow.

To everything there is a season,
a time for every purpose under heaven . . . .

Ecclesiastes 3:1 NKJV

A TIP FOR GUARDING YOUR HEART

Discovering God's purpose for your life is continuing education. God's plan is unfolding day by day. If you keep your eyes and your heart open, He'll reveal His plans. God has big things in store for you, but He may have quite a few lessons to teach you before you are fully prepared to do His will and fulfill His purposes.

WORDS OF WISDOM

Continually restate to yourself what the purpose of your life is.

Oswald Chambers

When God speaks to you through the Bible, prayer, circumstances, the church, or in some other way, he has a purpose in mind for your life.

Henry Blackaby and Claude King

Without God, life has no purpose, and without purpose, life has no meaning.

Rick Warren

Whatever purpose motivates your life, it must be something big enough and grand enough to make the investment worthwhile.

Warren Wiersbe

The worst thing that laziness does is rob a man of spiritual purpose.

Billy Graham

GOD'S WORDS OF WISDOM

Whatever you do, do all to the glory of God.

1 Corinthians 10:31 NKJV

You're sons of Light, daughters of Day. We live under wide open skies and know where we stand. So let's not sleepwalk through life . . .

1 Thessalonians 5:5-6 MSG

We look at this Son and see the God who cannot be seen. We look at this Son and see God's original purpose in everything created.

Colossians 1:15 MSG

There is one thing I always do. Forgetting the past and straining toward what is ahead, I keep trying to reach the goal and get the prize for which God called me . . . .

Philippians 3:13–14 NCV

SUMMING IT UP

When you gain a clear vision of your purpose for life here on earth—and for life everlasting—your steps will be sure.

GUARD YOUR STEPS BY WORSHIPPING GOD

Happy are those who hear the joyful call to worship,
for they will walk in the light of your presence, Lord.

Psalm 89:15 NLT

All of mankind is engaged in worship . . . of one kind or another. The question is not whether we worship, but what we worship. Some of us choose to worship God. The result is a plentiful harvest of joy, peace, and abundance. Others distance themselves from God by foolishly worshiping things of this earth such as fame, fortune, or personal gratification. To do so is a terrible mistake with eternal consequences.

Whenever we place our love for material possessions above our love for God—or when we yield to the countless temptations of this world—we find ourselves engaged in a struggle between good and evil, a clash between God and Satan. Our responses to these struggles have implications that echo throughout our families and throughout our communities.

How can we ensure that we cast our lot with God? We do so, in part, by the practice of regular worship in the company of fellow believers. When we worship God faithfully and fervently, we are blessed. When we fail to worship God, for whatever reason, we forfeit the spiritual gifts that He intends for us. Every day provides opportunities to put God where He belongs: at the center of our lives. When we do so, we worship not just with our words, but also with deeds, and that's as it should be. For believers, God comes first. Always first.

For it is written, "You shall worship the Lord your God, and Him only you shall serve."

Matthew 4:10 NKJV

A TIP FOR GUARDING YOUR HEART

Worship reminds you of the awesome power of God. So worship Him daily, and allow Him to work through you every day of the week (not just on Sundays).

WORDS OF WISDOM

I am of the opinion that we should not be concerned about working for God until we have learned the meaning and delight of worshipping Him.

A. W. Tozer

When God is at the center of your life, you worship. When he's not, you worry.

Rick Warren

Each time, before you intercede, be quiet first and worship God in His glory. Think of what He can do and how He delights to hear the prayers of His redeemed people. Think of your place and privilege in Christ, and expect great things!

Andrew Murray

Worship is spiritual. Our worship must be more than just outward expression, it must also take place in our spirits.

Franklin Graham

Inside the human heart is an undeniable, spiritual instinct to commune with its Creator.

Jim Cymbala

GOD'S WORDS OF WISDOM

A time is coming and has now come when the true worshipers will worship the Father in spirit and truth, for they are the kind of worshipers the Father seeks. God is spirit, and his worshipers must worship in spirit and in truth.

John 4:23-24 NIV

If any man thirst, let him come unto me, and drink.

John 7:37 KJV

But seek first his kingdom and his righteousness, and all these things will be given to you as well.

Matthew 6:33 NIV

God lifted him high and honored him far beyond anyone or anything, ever, so that all created beings in heaven and earth, even those long ago dead and buried, will bow in worship before this Jesus Christ, and call out in praise that he is the Master of all, to the glorious honor of God the Father.

Philippians 2:9-11 MSG

SUMMING IT UP

When you worship God with a sincere heart, He will guide your steps.

PART 4

GUARD
YOUR HEART

Above all else, guard your heart, for it affects
everything you do. Avoid all perverse talk;
stay far from corrupt speech. Look straight ahead,
and fix your eyes on what lies before you.
Mark out a straight path for your feet; then stick
to the path and stay safe. Don't get sidetracked;
keep your feet from following evil.

Proverbs 4:23 NLT

JESUS' PRINCIPLES OF PRAYER

*And when you pray, do not be like the hypocrites, for they
love to pray standing in the synagogues and on the street
corners to be seen by men. I tell you the truth, they have
received their reward in full. But when you pray, go into your
room, close the door and pray to your Father, who is unseen.
Then your Father, who sees what is done in secret, will reward
you. And when you pray, do not keep on babbling like pagans,
for they think they will be heard because of their many words.
Do not be like them, for your Father knows
what you need before you ask him.*

Matthew 6:5-8 NIV

If you sincerely wish to guard your heart, no discipline
is more important than the discipline of prayer. In the
sixth chapter of Matthew, Jesus offers the Bible's first
extensive instructions regarding prayer. It is here that Jesus
offers five principles about prayer that still apply.

Principle #1: Pray Regularly. Jesus began His lesson on prayer with the words, "And when you pray . . . " He did not say "if you pray." Prayer was assumed to be a regular daily activity for Christians. In truth, the Christian life cannot be maintained without consistent daily prayer.

Many Christians talk about their "prayer life." Yet God is not as interested in our having "prayer lives" as He is in our having "lives of prayer." And make no mistake: there's a big difference. A "prayer life" indicates that we divide our daily activities into times of prayer and times of non-prayer. What God prefers is that the entirety of a Christian's life should become a constant prayer lifted to Him—every activity dedicated to Him, every part of the day an act of worship.

Principle #2: Pray Privately. Jesus teaches that our times of protracted, concentrated prayer are not to be public spectacles, but are to be private. He admonishes us to go into our rooms, to close the door, and to talk to our Father who is unseen.

Does this mean that we are to never pray publicly? No, but it does mean that most of our prayers are to be private communications, just between God and us.

Some folks may say, "Well, I pray with my family." And, of course, that's an admirable activity. Others may say, "I am in a prayer group at church." And once again, God will be pleased. But nothing should obscure the fact that the majority of our concentrated prayer times are to be private.

Principle #3: Have a Time and Place for Prayer. What we schedule, we do. What we don't schedule, we may never get around to doing. So it's best to set aside a specific time for concentrated prayer.

Jesus had a set time of concentrated prayer—the early morning. Not a morning person? Then try the evening, or maybe during your lunch break. But whatever you do, have a regular, daily time of prayer . . . and have a place.

Jesus prayed outdoors; maybe you find that too distracting. If so, find a room where you can shut the door and pray. Do whatever works for you, but make certain that you have a specific place and time each day when you do nothing, absolutely nothing, but talk to the Father.

Principle #4: Prayer Is Rewarded. We sometimes baulk at the idea that we will be rewarded for doing what we consider to be our duty. Yet if Jesus did not want us to know about the rewards of prayer, He would not have told us that "your Father, who sees what is done in secret, will reward you" (Matthew 6:6).

Do these rewards come now or later? Of course, there may be many earthly rewards for prayer; and we most assuredly benefit from the blessings that arise from the act of praying. But we can also be certain that our prayers will be rewarded in heaven.

Principle #5: Keep It Simple. Jesus said that we are not to pray, "babbling like pagans, for they think they will be heard because of their many words." He tells us that our Father knows what we need before we ask Him. So, we can keep our prayers short, sweet, and simple. We needn't try to impress God by fancy speeches or lengthy lectures. God isn't concerned with the eloquence of our words, which, by the way, is a very good thing. That means that all of us can talk intimately with God . . . and He always understands.

A TIP FOR GUARDING YOUR HEART

Pray early and often. One way to make sure that your heart is in tune with God is to pray often. The more you talk to God, the more He will talk to you.

WORDS OF WISDOM

Prayer is never the least we can do; it is always the most!

A.W. Tozer

Pour out your heart to God and tell Him how you feel. Be real, be honest, and when you get it all out, you'll start to feel the gradual covering of God's comforting presence.

Bill Hybels

I live in the spirit of prayer; I pray as I walk, when I lie down, and when I rise. And, the answers are always coming.

George Mueller

Prayer connects us with God's limitless potential.

Henry Blackaby

It is impossible to overstate the need for prayer in the fabric of family life.

James Dobson

GOD'S WORDS OF WISDOM

"'Relax, Daniel,' he continued, 'don't be afraid. From the moment you decided to humble yourself to receive understanding, your prayer was heard, and I set out to come to you.'"

Daniel 10:12 MSG

I want men everywhere to lift up holy hands in prayer, without anger or disputing.

1 Timothy 2:8 NIV

If my people who are called by my name, will humble themselves and pray and seek my face and turn from their wicked ways, then will I hear from heaven and will forgive their sin and will heal their land.

2 Chronicles 7:14 NIV

I sought the LORD, and he heard me, and delivered me from all my fears.

Psalm 34:4 KJV

SUMMING IT UP

Prayer changes things—and you—so pray.

GUARD YOUR HEART WITH MOUNTAIN-MOVING FAITH

For truly I say to you, if you have faith as a mustard seed,
you shall say to this mountain,
"Move from here to there" and it shall move;
and nothing shall be impossible to you.

Matthew 17:20 NASB

Every life (including yours) can be a grand adventure in faithful living . . . or not. And, every day (including this one) presents the opportunity to trust God faithfully . . . or to ignore Him altogether. The decision to trust God is yours, and so are the consequences of that decision.

Your life, like every life, is a series of successes and failures, celebrations and disappointments, joys and sorrows. Every step of the way, through every triumph and tragedy, God will stand by your side and strengthen you . . .

if you have faith in Him. Jesus taught His disciples that if they had faith, they could move mountains. You can too.

How can you strengthen your faith? Through praise, through worship, through Bible study, and through prayer. And, as your faith becomes stronger, you will find ways to share it with your friends, your family, and with the world. When you place your faith, your trust, indeed your life in the hands of Christ Jesus, you'll be amazed at the marvelous things He can do with you and through you; so trust God's plans. With Him, all things are possible, and He stands ready to open a world of possibilities to you . . . if you have faith.

Today, you may face challenges that leave you discouraged or exhausted. If so, remember this: whatever your challenge, whatever your trouble, God can handle it. And will. Just place your faith in Him, and then, with no further ado, let the mountain-moving begin.

A Tip for Guarding Your Heart

Don't be embarrassed to discuss your faith. You need not have attended seminary to have worthwhile opinions about your faith. Express those opinions.

WORDS OF WISDOM

There are a lot of things in life that are difficult to understand. Faith allows the soul to go beyond what the eyes can see.

John Maxwell

The popular idea of faith is of a certain obstinate optimism: the hope, tenaciously held in the face of trouble, that the universe is fundamentally friendly and things may get better.

J. I. Packer

I am truly grateful that faith enables me to move past the question of "Why?"

Zig Ziglar

When you enroll in the "school of faith," you never know what may happen next. The life of faith presents challenges that keep you going—and keep you growing!

Warren Wiersbe

Nothing is more disastrous than to study faith, analyze faith, make noble resolves of faith, but never actually to make the leap of faith.

Vance Havner

GOD'S WORDS OF WISDOM

Be on the alert, stand firm in the faith, act like men, be strong.

1 Corinthians 16:13 NASB

For whatever is born of God overcomes the world. And this is the victory that has overcome the world—our faith.

1 John 5:4 NKJV

Fight the good fight of faith; take hold of the eternal life to which you were called . . . .

1 Timothy 6:12 NASB

I have fought the good fight, I have finished the race, I have kept the faith.

2 Timothy 4:7 NIV

SUMMING IT UP

If your faith is strong enough, you and God—working together—can move mountains.

ABOVE ALL ELSE GUARD YOUR HEART

Above all else, guard your heart,
for it affects everything you do.

Proverbs 4:23 NLT

Oswald Chambers, the author of the Christian classic devotional text, *My Utmost For His Highest*, advised, "Never support an experience which does not have God as its source, and faith in God as its result." These words serve as a powerful reminder that, as Christians, we are called to walk with God and obey His commandments. But, we live in a world that presents us with countless temptations to stray far from God's path. We Christians, when confronted with sin, have clear instructions: Walk—or better yet run—in the opposite direction.

When we seek righteousness in our own lives—and when we seek the companionship of those who do likewise—we not only build our characters, but we also reap the spiritual rewards that God offers those who obey

Him. When we live righteously and according to God's commandments, He blesses us in ways that we cannot fully understand.

Each new day presents countless opportunities to put God in first place . . . or not. When we honor Him by living according to His commandments, we earn for ourselves the abundance and peace that He promises. But, when we concern ourselves more with pleasing others than with pleasing our Creator—or when we allow ourselves to be overwhelmed by the temptations that surround us—we bring needless suffering upon ourselves and our families.

Would you like a time-tested formula for character building and a not-so-secret secret for successful living? Here it is: Seek God's approval in every aspect of your life. Does this sound too simple? Perhaps it is simple, but it is also the only way to reap the marvelous riches that God has in store for you.

So today, take every step of your journey with God as your traveling companion. Read His Word and follow His commandments. Support only those activities that honor your Creator and your character. Be an example of righteous living to your friends and neighbors. And guard your heart against the inevitable temptations of everyday life. Then, reap the blessings that God has promised to all those who live according to His will and His Word.

WORDS OF WISDOM

We must appropriate the tender mercy of God every day after conversion, or problems quickly develop. We need his grace daily in order to live a righteous life.

Jim Cymbala

A man who lives right, and is right, has more power in his silence than another has by his words.

Phillips Brooks

Trusting God is the bottom line of Christian righteousness.

R. C. Sproul

Sanctify yourself and you will sanctify society.

St. Francis of Assisi

A TIP FOR GUARDING YOUR HEART

Today, consider the value of living a life that is pleasing to God. And while you're at it, think about the rewards that are likely to be yours when you do the right thing day in and day out.

GOD'S WORDS OF WISDOM

For the eyes of the Lord are on the righteous, and His ears are open to their prayers; but the face of the Lord is against those who do evil.

1 Peter 3:12 NKJV

Walk in a manner worthy of the God who calls you into His own kingdom and glory.

1 Thessalonians 2:12 NASB

Discipline yourself for the purpose of godliness.

1 Timothy 4:7 NASB

Run away from infantile indulgence. Run after mature righteousness—faith, love, peace—joining those who are in honest and serious prayer before God.

2 Timothy 2:22 MSG

SUMMING IT UP

Because God is just, He rewards righteousness just as surely as He punishes sin.

GUARD YOUR HEART BY LIVING COURAGEOUSLY

Wait for the Lord; be courageous and let your heart be strong.
Wait for the Lord.

Psalm 27:14 Holman CSB

Every life (including yours) is an unfolding series of events: some fabulous, some not-so-fabulous, and some downright disheartening. When you reach the mountaintops of life, praising God is easy. But, when the storm clouds form overhead, your faith will be tested, sometimes to the breaking point. As a believer, you can take comfort in this fact: Wherever you find yourself, whether at the top of the mountain or the depths of the valley, God is there, and because He cares for you, you can live courageously.

Believing Christians have every reason to be courageous. After all, the ultimate battle has already been fought and won on the cross at Calvary. But, even dedicated followers of Christ may find their courage tested by the inevitable disappointments and tragedies that occur in the lives of believers and non-believers alike.

The next time you find your courage tested to the limit, guard your heart by remembering that God is as near as your next breath. And remember that He is your shield and your strength. Call upon Him in your hour of need and then be comforted. Whatever your challenge, whatever your trouble, God can handle it. And will.

A TIP FOR GUARDING YOUR HEART

With God as your partner, you have nothing to fear. Why? Because you and God, working together, can handle absolutely anything that comes your way. So the next time you'd like an extra measure of courage, recommit yourself to a true one-on-one relationship with your Creator. When you sincerely turn to Him, He will never fail you.

WORDS OF WISDOM

Jesus Christ can make the weakest man into a divine dreadnought, fearing nothing.

Oswald Chambers

Fill your mind with thoughts of God rather than thoughts of fear.

Norman Vincent Peale

Faith not only can help you through a crisis, it can help you to approach life after the hard times with a whole new perspective. It can help you adopt an outlook of hope and courage through faith to face reality.

John Maxwell

Dreaming the dream of God is not for cowards.

Joey Johnson

Take courage. We walk in the wilderness today and in the Promised Land tomorrow.

D. L. Moody

GOD'S WORDS OF WISDOM

Be strong and courageous, and do the work. Don't be afraid or discouraged by the size of the task, for the LORD God, my God, is with you. He will not fail you or forsake you.

1 Chronicles 28:20 NLT

Therefore, being always of good courage . . . we walk by faith, not by sight.

2 Corinthians 5:6-7 NASB

God doesn't want us to be shy with his gifts, but bold and loving and sensible.

2 Timothy 1:7 MSG

But Moses said to the people, "Do not fear! Stand by and see the salvation of the LORD."

Exodus 14:13 NASB

SUMMING IT UP

If you are a disciple of the risen Christ, you have every reason on earth—and in heaven—to live courageously. And that's precisely what you should do.

GUARD YOUR HEART WITH BIBLE STUDY

All Scripture is inspired by God and is profitable for teaching,
for rebuking, for correcting, for training in righteousness,
so that the man of God may be complete,
equipped for every good work.

2 Timothy 3:16-17 Holman CSB

The Bible is unlike any other book. A. W. Tozer wrote, "The purpose of the Bible is to bring men to Christ, to make them holy and prepare them for heaven. In this it is unique among books, and it always fulfills its purpose."

As Christians, we are called upon to share God's Holy Word with a world in desperate need of His healing hand. The Bible is a priceless gift, a tool for Christians to use as they share the Good News of their Savior, Christ Jesus. Too many Christians, however, keep their spiritual tool kits tightly closed and out of sight.

Jonathan Edwards advised, "Be assiduous in reading the Holy Scriptures. This is the fountain whence all knowledge in divinity must be derived. Therefore let not this treasure lie by you neglected." God's Holy Word is, indeed, a priceless, one-of-a-kind treasure. Handle it with care, but more importantly, handle it every day.

*Blessed are those who hunger
and thirst for righteousness,
for they will be filled.*

Matthew 5:6 NIV

A TIP FOR GUARDING YOUR HEART

Wisdom is found in God's Word. Seek to gain God's wisdom through daily Bible readings.

WORDS OF WISDOM

It takes calm, thoughtful, prayerful meditation on the Word to extract its deepest nourishment.

Vance Havner

When you read God's Word, you must constantly be saying to yourself, "It is talking to me about me."

Søren Kierkegaard

The promises of Scripture are not mere pious hopes or sanctified guesses. They are more than sentimental words to be printed on decorated cards for Sunday School children. They are eternal verities. They are true. There is no perhaps about them.

Peter Marshall

God has given us all sorts of counsel and direction in his written Word; thank God, we have it written down in black and white.

John Eldredge

God has spoken by His prophets, spoken His unchanging Word, each from age to age proclaiming God, the one, the righteous Lord.

George W. Briggs

GOD'S WORDS OF WISDOM

Every word of God is pure: he is a shield unto them that put their trust in him.

Proverbs 30:5 KJV

For the word of God is quick, and powerful, and sharper than any two-edged sword, piercing even to the dividing asunder of soul and spirit, and of the joints and marrow, and is a discerner of the thoughts and intents of the heart.

Hebrews 4:12 KJV

Jesus answered and said unto him, If a man love me, he will keep my words: and my Father will love him, and we will come unto him, and make our abode with him.

John 14:23 KJV

Heaven and earth will pass away, but my words will never pass away.

Matthew 24:35 NIV

SUMMING IT UP

God's Word can guide your steps and guard your heart. Let your Bible be your guide.

GUARD YOUR STEPS BY OVERCOMING YOUR MISTAKES

Even though good people may be bothered
by trouble seven times, they are never defeated.

Proverbs 24:16 NCV

When you experience failure, you must guard your heart. And make no mistake: you will experience failure. Life's occasional setbacks are simply the price that we all must pay for our willingness to take risks as we follow our dreams. But even when we encounter bitter disappointments, we must never lose faith.

Hebrews 10:36 advises, "Patient endurance is what you need now, so you will continue to do God's will. Then you will receive all that he has promised" (NLT). These words remind us that when we persevere, we will eventually receive the rewards which God has promised us. What's required is perseverance, not perfection.

When we face hardships, God stands ready to protect us. Our responsibility, of course, is to ask Him for protection. When we call upon Him in heartfelt prayer, He will answer—in His own time and according to His own plan—and He will do His part to heal us. We, of course, must do our part, too.

And, while we are waiting for God's plans to unfold and for His healing touch to restore us, we can be comforted in the knowledge that our Creator can overcome any obstacle, even if we cannot.

A TIP FOR GUARDING YOUR HEART

Failure isn't permanent . . . unless you fail to get up. So pick yourself up, dust yourself off, and trust God. He will make it right. Warren Wiersbe had this advice: "No matter how badly we have failed, we can always get up and begin again. Our God is the God of new beginnings." And don't forget: the best time to begin again is now.

WORDS OF WISDOM

If you learn from a defeat, you have not really lost.

Zig Ziglar

As long as a man keeps his faith in God and in himself nothing can permanently defeat him.

Wilferd Peterson

Do not be one of those who, rather than risk failure, never attempt anything.

Thomas Merton

Success or failure can be pretty well predicted by the degree to which the heart is fully in it.

John Eldredge

God is a specialist; He is well able to work our failures into His plans. Often the doorway to success is entered through the hallway of failure.

Erwin Lutzer

GOD'S WORDS OF WISDOM

If we confess our sins to him, he is faithful and just to forgive us and to cleanse us from every wrong.

1 John 1:9 NLT

If you hide your sins, you will not succeed. If you confess and reject them, you will receive mercy.

Proverbs 28:13 NCV

If you listen to constructive criticism, you will be at home among the wise.

Proverbs 15:31 NLT

I waited patiently for the LORD; he turned to me and heard my cry. He lifted me out of the slimy pit, out of the mud and mire; he set my feet on a rock and gave me a firm place to stand. He put a new song in my mouth, a hymn of praise to our God . . . .

Psalm 40:1-3 NIV

SUMMING IT UP

Setbacks are inevitable—your response to them is optional. You can turn your stumbling blocks into stepping stones . . . and you should.

GUARD YOUR HEART BY SENSING GOD'S PRESENCE

Draw near to God, and He will draw near to you.

James 4:8 Holman CSB

Since God is everywhere, we are free to sense His presence whenever we take the time to quiet our souls and turn our prayers to Him. But sometimes, amid the incessant demands of life, we turn our thoughts far from God; when we do, we suffer.

Do you schedule a regular meeting each day with your Creator? You should. During these moments of stillness, you will gain direction, perspective, and peace—God's peace.

The comforting words of Psalm 46:10 remind us to "Be still, and know that I am God." When we do so, we sense the loving presence of our Heavenly Father, and we are comforted by the certain knowledge that God is not far away . . . and He isn't even nearby. He is, quite literally, here. And it's up to each of us to sense His presence.

For the eyes of the Lord range throughout the earth to strengthen those whose hearts are fully committed to him.

2 Chronicles 16:9 NIV

A TIP FOR GUARDING YOUR HEART

Having trouble hearing God? If so, slow yourself down, tune out the distractions, and listen carefully. God has important things to say; your task is to be still and listen.

Words of Wisdom

The Lord Jesus by His Holy Spirit is with me, and the knowledge of His presence dispels the darkness and allays any fears.

Bill Bright

Whatever we have done in the past, be it good or evil, great or small, is irrelevant to our stance before God today. It is only now that we are in the presence of God.

Brennan Manning

The world, space, and all visible components reverberate with God's Presence and demonstrate His Mighty Power.

Franklin Graham

God still draws near to us in the ordinary, commonplace, everyday experience and places. He comes in surprising ways.

Henry Gariepy

I have a capacity in my soul for taking in God entirely. I am as sure as I live that nothing is so near to me as God. God is nearer to me than I am to myself; my existence depends on the nearness and the presence of God.

Meister Eckhart

GOD'S WORDS OF WISDOM

No, I will not abandon you as orphans—I will come to you.

John 14:18 NLT

Again, this is God's command: to believe in his personally named Son, Jesus Christ. He told us to love each other, in line with the original command. As we keep his commands, we live deeply and surely in him, and he lives in us. And this is how we experience his deep and abiding presence in us: by the Spirit he gave us.

1 John 3:23-24 MSG

You will seek Me and find Me when you search for Me with all your heart.

Jeremiah 29:13 Holman CSB

God did this so that men would seek him and perhaps reach out for him and find him, though he is not far from each one of us.

Acts 17:27 NIV

SUMMING IT UP

God isn't far away. He's right here, right now.

GUARD YOUR HEART BY COUNTING YOUR BLESSINGS

Blessings are on the head of the righteous.

Proverbs 10:6 Holman CSB

If you sat down and began counting your blessings, how long would it take? A very, very long time! Your blessings include life, freedom, family, friends, talents, and possessions, for starters. But, your greatest blessing—a gift that is yours for the asking—is God's gift of salvation through Christ Jesus.

Are you a thankful believer who takes time each day to take a partial inventory of the gifts God has given you? Hopefully you are that kind of Christian. After all, God's Word makes it clear: a wise heart is a thankful heart.

We honor God, in part, by the genuine gratitude we feel in our hearts for the blessings He has bestowed upon us. Yet even the most saintly among us must endure periods of fear, doubt, and regret. Why? Because we are imperfect human beings who are incapable of perfect gratitude. Still, even on life's darker days, we must seek to cleanse our hearts of negative emotions and fill them, instead, with praise, with love, with hope, and with thanksgiving. To do otherwise is to be unfair to ourselves, to our loved ones, and to our God.

Sometimes, life-here-on-earth can be complicated, demanding, and frustrating. When the demands of life leave us rushing from place to place with scarcely a moment to spare, we may fail to pause and thank our Creator for His gifts. But, whenever we neglect to give proper thanks to the Father, we suffer because of our misplaced priorities.

Today, begin making a list of your blessings. You most certainly will not be able to make a complete list, but take a few moments and jot down as many blessings as you can. Then, give thanks to the Giver of all good things: God. His love for you is eternal, as are His gifts. And it's never too soon—or too late—to offer Him thanks.

A Tip for Guarding Your Heart

Carve out time to thank God for His blessings. Take time out of every day (not just on Sundays) to praise God and thank Him for His gifts.

WORDS OF WISDOM

Grace is an outrageous blessing bestowed freely on a totally undeserving recipient.

Bill Hybels

God's love for His children is unconditional, no strings attached. But, God's blessings on our lives do come with a condition—obedience. If we are to receive the fullness of God's blessings, we must obey Him and keep His commandments.

Jim Gallery

With the goodness of God to desire our highest welfare and the wisdom of God to plan it, what do we lack? Surely we are the most favored of all creatures.

A. W. Tozer

It is when we give ourselves to be a blessing that we can specially count on the blessing of God.

Andrew Murray

GOD'S WORDS OF WISDOM

You will show me the path of life; in Your presence is fullness of joy; at Your right hand are pleasures forevermore.

Psalm 16:11 NKJV

For surely, O LORD, you bless the righteous; you surround them with your favor as with a shield.

Psalm 5:12 NIV

The Lord is kind and merciful, slow to get angry, full of unfailing love. The Lord is good to everyone. He showers compassion on all his creation.

Psalm 145:8-9 NLT

Blessed is a man who endures trials, because when he passes the test he will receive the crown of life that He has promised to those who love Him.

James 1:12 Holman CSB

SUMMING IT UP

God has given you more blessings than you can count. You job is to accept them and be grateful.

GUARD YOUR HEART WITH A POSITIVE ATTITUDE

Finally, brethren, whatever things are true, whatever things are noble, whatever things are just, whatever things are pure, whatever things are lovely, whatever things are of good report, if there is any virtue and if there is anything praiseworthy— meditate on these things.

Philippians 4:8 NKJV

The Christian life is a cause for celebration, but sometimes we don't feel much like celebrating. In fact, when the weight of the world seems to bear down upon our shoulders, celebration may be the last thing on our minds . . . but it shouldn't be. As God's children, we are all blessed beyond measure on good days and bad. This day is a non-renewable resource—once it's gone, it's gone forever. We should give thanks for this day while using it for the glory of God.

What will be your attitude today? Will you be fearful, angry, bored, or worried? Will you be cynical, bitter, or pessimistic? If so, God wants to have a little talk with you.

God wants you to guard your heart with a positive, upbeat, thankful attitude. He created you in His own image, and He wants you to experience joy and abundance. But, God will not force His joy upon you; you must claim it for yourself. So today, and every day hereafter, celebrate the life that God has given you. Think optimistically about yourself and your future. Give thanks to the One who has given you everything, and trust in your heart that He wants to give you so much more.

> *Set your mind on things above,*
> *not on things on the earth.*
>
> *Colossians 3:2 NKJV*

A TIP FOR GUARDING YOUR HEART

Attitudes are contagious, so it's important to associate with people who are upbeat, optimistic, and encouraging.

WORDS OF WISDOM

Attitude is more important than the past, than education, than money, than circumstances, than what people do or say. It is more important than appearance, giftedness, or skill.

Charles Swindoll

You've heard the saying, "Life is what you make it." That means we have a choice. We can choose to have a life full of frustration and fear, but we can just as easily choose one of joy and contentment.

Dennis Swanberg

Do you wonder where you can go for encouragement and motivation? Run to Jesus.

Max Lucado

I have witnessed many attitudes make a positive turnaround through prayer.

John Maxwell

It's your choice: you can either count your blessings or recount your disappointments.

Jim Gallery

GOD'S WORDS OF WISDOM

*Come near to God, and God will come near to you. You
sinners, clean sin out of your lives. You who are trying to
follow God and the world at the same time, make your thinking
pure.*

James 4:8 NCV

*Those who are pure in their thinking are happy, because they
will be with God.*

Matthew 5:8 NCV

So prepare your minds for service and have self-control.

1 Peter 1:13 NCV

*You were taught, with regard to your former way of life, to
put off your old self, which is being corrupted by its deceitful
desires; to be made new in the attitude of your minds; and to
put on the new self, created to be like God in true righteousness
and holiness.*

Ephesians 4:22-24 NIV

SUMMING IT UP

A positive attitude leads to positive results; a negative
attitude leads elsewhere.

GUARD YOUR HEART BY ACCEPTING GOD'S PEACE

The peace of God, which surpasses all understanding,
will guard your hearts and minds through Christ Jesus.

Philippians 4:7 NKJV

Have you found the genuine peace that can be yours through a passionate commitment to Jesus Christ? Or are you still rushing after the illusion of "peace and happiness" that the world promises but cannot deliver? The beautiful words of John 14:27 remind us that Jesus offers us peace, not as the world gives, but as He alone gives: "Peace I leave with you. My peace I give to you. I do not give to you as the world gives. Your heart must not be troubled or fearful" (Holman CSB). Our challenge is to accept Christ's peace into our hearts and then, as best we can, to share His peace with our neighbors.

Are you at peace with the direction of your life? If you're a Christian, you should be. Perhaps you seek a new direction or a sense of renewed purpose, but those feelings should never rob you of the genuine peace that can and should be yours through a personal relationship with Jesus. The demands of everyday living should never obscure the fact that Christ died so that you might have life abundant and eternal.

Today, as a gift to yourself, to your family, and to your friends, claim the inner peace that is your spiritual birthright: the peace of Jesus Christ. It is offered freely; it has been paid for in full; it is yours for the asking. So ask. And then share.

God has called us to live in peace.

1 Corinthians 7:15 NIV

A TIP FOR GUARDING YOUR HEART

Do you want to discover God's peace? Then do your best to live in the center of God's will.

WORDS OF WISDOM

The better acquainted you become with God, the less tension you feel and the more peace you possess.

Charles Allen

A great many people are trying to make peace, but that has already been done. God has not left it for us to do; all we have to do is to enter into it.

D. L. Moody

For Jesus peace seems to have meant not the absence of struggle but the presence of love.

Frederick Buechner

The Christian has a deep, silent, hidden peace, which the world sees not, like some well in a retired and shady place.

John Henry Cardinal Newman

That peace, which has been described and which believers enjoy, is a participation of the peace which their glorious Lord and Master himself enjoys.

Jonathan Edwards

GOD'S WORDS OF WISDOM

And let the peace of God rule in your hearts . . . and be ye thankful.

Colossians 3:15 KJV

You will keep in perfect peace him whose mind is steadfast, because he trusts in you.

Isaiah 26:3 NIV

I have told you these things, so that in me you may have peace. In this world you will have trouble. But take heart! I have overcome the world.

John 16:33 NIV

Those who love Your law have great peace, and nothing causes them to stumble.

Psalm 119:165 NASB

SUMMING IT UP

God offers peace that passes human understanding . . . and He wants you to make His peace your peace.

GUARD YOUR HEART BY USING GOD'S GIFTS

Do not neglect the gift that is in you.

1 Timothy 4:14 Holman CSB

The old saying is both familiar and true: "What we are is God's gift to us; what we become is our gift to God." Each of us possesses special talents, gifted by God, that can be nurtured carefully or ignored totally. Sometimes, we don't fully recognize our own talents, and, sometimes, we don't fully appreciate the gifts we've been given. That's when we need the insights, the support, and the encouragement of trusted friends.

Oswald Chambers observed, "A friend is one who makes me do my best." How true. Our most trusted friends encourage us to set our sights where they need to be set: high. We can do the same for them, and should.

God didn't create us to be mediocre. He gave us talents so that we might use them to the full. So, if you're coasting along in neutral, it's time to shift into a higher gear. And, if you know someone whose talents are underused, remind him that those talents are priceless gifts from God, and the way that we say "thank you" for God's gifts is to use them.

I remind you to fan into flame the gift of God.

2 Timothy 1:6 NIV

A TIP FOR GUARDING YOUR HEART

You are the sole owner of your own set of talents and opportunities. God has given you your own particular gifts—the rest is up to you.

WORDS OF WISDOM

Employ whatever God has entrusted you with, in doing good, all possible good, in every possible kind and degree.

John Wesley

If you want to reach your potential, you need to add a strong work ethic to your talent.

John Maxwell

God often reveals His direction for our lives through the way He made us . . . with a certain personality and unique skills.

Bill Hybels

What we are is God's gift to us. What we become is our gift to God.

Anonymous

One thing taught large in the Holy Scriptures is that while God gives His gifts freely, He will require a strict accounting of them at the end of the road. Each man is personally responsible for his store, be it large or small, and will be required to explain his use of it before the judgment seat of Christ.

A. W. Tozer

GOD'S WORDS OF WISDOM

God has given gifts to each of you from his great variety of spiritual gifts. Manage them well so that God's generosity can flow through you.

1 Peter 4:10 NLT

Now there are varieties of gifts, but the same Spirit. And there are varieties of ministries, and the same Lord.

1 Corinthians 12:4-5 NASB

The man who had received the five talents brought the other five. "Master," he said, "you entrusted me with five talents. See, I have gained five more." His master replied, "Well done, good and faithful servant! You have been faithful with a few things; I will put you in charge of many things. Come and share your master's happiness."

Matthew 25:20-21 NIV

SUMMING IT UP

God has given you a unique array of talents and opportunities. The rest is up to you.

GUARD YOUR HEART WHEN THINGS GO WRONG

A man's heart plans his way, but the Lord determines his steps.

Proverbs 16:9 Holman CSB

When things go wrong, it's easy to become discouraged. But a far better strategy is this: Work to change the things you can, and trust God to handle the rest. But that may not be easy. If you're like most men, you like being in control. Period. You want things to happen according to your wishes and according to your timetable. But sometimes, God has other plans . . . and He always has the final word.

The American theologian Reinhold Niebuhr composed a profoundly simple verse that came to be known as the Serenity Prayer: "God, grant me the serenity to accept the things I cannot change, the courage to change the things I can, and the wisdom to know the difference." Niebuhr's words are far easier to recite than they are to live by.

Author Hannah Whitall Smith observed, "How changed our lives would be if we could only fly through the days on wings of surrender and trust!" These words remind us that even when we cannot understand the workings of God, we must trust Him and accept His will.

So if you've encountered unfortunate circumstances that are beyond your power to control, accept those circumstances . . . and trust God. When you do, you can be comforted in the knowledge that your Creator is both loving and wise, and that He understands His plans perfectly, even when you do not.

Give in to God, come to terms with him and everything will turn out just fine.

Job 22:21 MSG

A TIP FOR GUARDING YOUR HEART

Acceptance means learning to trust God more. Today, think of at least one aspect of your life that you've been reluctant to accept, and then prayerfully ask God to help you trust Him more by accepting the past.

WORDS OF WISDOM

In the kingdom of God, the surest way to lose something is to try to protect it, and the best way to keep it is to let it go.

A. W. Tozer

Acceptance is resting in God's goodness, believing that He has all things under His control.

Charles Swindoll

Sometimes the greatest act of faith is not to ask for a miracle.

Henry Blackaby

The more comfortable we are with mystery in our journey, the more rest we will know along the way.

John Eldredge

Tomorrow's job is fathered by today's acceptance. Acceptance of what, at least for the moment, you cannot alter.

Max Lucado

GOD'S WORDS OF WISDOM

Shall I not drink from the cup the Father has given me?

John 18:11 NLT

He is the Lord. Let him do what he thinks is best.

1 Samuel 3:18 NCV

The Lord says, "Forget what happened before, and do not think about the past. Look at the new thing I am going to do. It is already happening. Don't you see it? I will make a road in the desert and rivers in the dry land."

Isaiah 43:18-19 NCV

He said, "I came naked from my mother's womb, and I will be stripped of everything when I die. The LORD gave me everything I had, and the LORD has taken it away. Praise the name of the LORD!"

Job 1:21 NLT

SUMMING IT UP

When you encounter situations that you cannot change, you must learn the wisdom of acceptance . . . and you must learn to trust God.

GUARD YOUR HEART AGAINST WORRY

Don't worry about anything, but in everything,
through prayer and petition with thanksgiving,
let your requests be made known to God.

Philippians 4:6 Holman CSB

Because we are imperfect human beings struggling with imperfect circumstances, we worry. Even though we, as Christians, have the assurance of salvation—even though we, as Christians, have the promise of God's love and protection—we find ourselves fretting over the inevitable frustrations of everyday life. Jesus understood our concerns when He spoke the reassuring words found in the 6th chapter of Matthew.

Where is the best place to take your worries? Take them to God. Take your troubles to Him; take your fears to Him; take your doubts to Him; take your weaknesses to Him; take your sorrows to Him . . . and leave them all there. Seek protection from the One who offers you eternal salvation; build your spiritual house upon the Rock that cannot be moved.

Perhaps you are concerned about your future, your health, or your finances. Or perhaps you are simply a "worrier" by nature. If so, make Matthew 6 a regular part of your daily Bible reading. This beautiful passage will remind you that God still sits in His heaven and you are His beloved child. Then, perhaps, you will worry a little less and trust God a little more, and that's as it should be because God is trustworthy . . . and you are protected.

I was very worried, but you comforted me . . . .

Psalm 94:19 NCV

A Tip for Guarding Your Heart

An important part of becoming a more mature Christian is learning to worry less and to trust God more. And while you're at it, remember that worry is never a valid substitute for work. So do your best, and then turn your worries over to God.

WORDS OF WISDOM

The beginning of anxiety is the end of faith, and the beginning of true faith is the end of anxiety.

George Mueller

God is bigger than your problems. Whatever worries press upon you today, put them in God's hands and leave them there.

Billy Graham

Today is the tomorrow we worried about yesterday.

Dennis Swanberg

This life of faith, then, consists in just this—being a child in the Father's house. Let the ways of childish confidence and freedom from care, which so please you and win your heart when you observe your own little ones, teach you what you should be in your attitude toward God.

Hannah Whitall Smith

Pray, and let God worry.

Martin Luther

GOD'S WORDS OF WISDOM

*So do not worry, saying, "What shall we eat?" or "What shall
we drink?" or "What shall we wear?" For the pagans run after
all these things, and your heavenly Father knows that you need
them. But seek first his kingdom and his righteousness, and
all these things will be given to you as well. Therefore do not
worry about tomorrow, for tomorrow will worry about itself.
Each day has enough trouble of its own.*

Matthew 6:31-34 NIV

*Come to Me, all you who labor and are heavy laden, and I will
give you rest. Take My yoke upon you and learn from Me, for
I am gentle and lowly in heart, and you will find rest for your
souls. For My yoke is easy and My burden is light.*

Matthew 11:28-30 NKJV

An anxious heart weighs a man down . . . .

Proverbs 12:25 NIV

SUMMING IT UP

You have worries, but God has solutions. Your
challenge is to trust Him to solve the problems that you
can't.

ABOVE ALL ELSE: YOUR RELATIONSHIP WITH CHRIST

For God so loved the world that he gave his only Son,
so that everyone who believes in him will
not perish but have eternal life.

John 3:16 NLT

Eternal life is not an event that begins when you die. Eternal life begins when you invite Jesus into your heart right here on earth. So it's important to remember that God's plans for you are not limited to the ups and downs of everyday life. If you've allowed Jesus to reign over your heart, you've already begun your eternal journey.

As mere mortals, our vision for the future, like our lives here on earth, is limited. God's vision is not burdened by such limitations: His plans extend throughout all eternity.

Let us praise the Creator for His priceless gift, and let us share the Good News with all who cross our paths. We return our Father's love by accepting His grace and by sharing His message and His love. When we do, we are blessed here on earth and throughout all eternity.

I have written these things to you who believe
in the name of the Son of God,
so that you may know that you have eternal life.

1 John 5:13 Holman CSB

A TIP FOR GUARDING YOUR HEART

Your eternity with God is secure because of your belief in Jesus.

WORDS OF WISDOM

Teach us to set our hopes on heaven, to hold firmly to the promise of eternal life, so that we can withstand the struggles and storms of this world.

Max Lucado

Christ is the only liberator whose liberation lasts forever.

Malcolm Muggeridge

Those of us who know the wonderful grace of redemption look forward to an eternity with God, when all things will be made new, when all our longings will at last find ultimate and final satisfaction.

Joseph Stowell

And because we know Christ is alive, we have hope for the present and hope for life beyond the grave.

Billy Graham

The damage done to us on this earth will never find its way into that safe city. We can relax, we can rest, and though some of us can hardly imagine it, we can prepare to feel safe and secure for all of eternity.

Bill Hybels

GOD'S WORDS OF WISDOM

And this is the testimony: God has given us eternal life, and this life is in His Son. The one who has the Son has life. The one who doesn't have the Son of God does not have life.

1 John 5:11-12 Holman CSB

Jesus said to her, "I am the resurrection and the life. The one who believes in Me, even if he dies, will live. Everyone who lives and believes in Me will never die—ever. Do you believe this?"

John 11:25-26 Holman CSB

Pursue righteousness, godliness, faith, love, endurance, and gentleness. Fight the good fight for the faith; take hold of eternal life, to which you were called and have made a good confession before many witnesses.

1 Timothy 6:11-12 Holman CSB

SUMMING IT UP

God offers you a priceless gift: the gift of eternal life. If you have not already done so, accept God's gift today—tomorrow may be too late.

Tim Way has been on staff with Family Christian Stores for the past twenty-three years. He is currently the Senior Buyer of Book, Bibles, and Church Resources. Tim and his wife, Ramona, live in Grand Rapids, Michigan. They have three grown children and three grandchildren.

Dr. Criswell Freeman is a best-selling author with over 14,000,000 books in print. He is a graduate of Vanderbilt University. He received his doctoral degree from the Adler School of Professional Psychology in Chicago; he also attended classes at Southern Seminary in Louisville where he was mentored by the late Wayne Oates, a pioneer in the field of pastoral counseling. Dr. Freeman is married; he has two children.